DATE DUE

THE
NEW ENGLISH

THE
NEW ENGLISH

William Chisholm

FUNK & WAGNALLS NEW YORK 1969

This book is dedicated, like, with love,
to two nifty girls, Marian and Susan,
and to two dandy boys, Jim and Tom

CONTENTS

INTRODUCTION

In matters of education Americans often tend to be conscious innovators and experimentalists but unconscious traditionalists. We are bold in developing and trying out new formats. Indeed, we are almost forced into doing so by the heterogeneity of our educational population. Very often, however, the change does not penetrate beneath the surface; the fundamental ideas, the basic philosophy remain unaltered. It might be described as putting old wine into new bottles.

As a consequence of all this, whenever the word "new" is used in connection with any school subject, it cannot be accepted at its face value. We must try to determine just what is new about it, what the newness consists of. For example, the New Math does employ concepts which have hitherto been reserved for the advanced mathematician. The newness of the New Physics consists rather of a different organization of subject matter, a change in emphasis. Foreign languages in the new key stress a different approach in teaching method. This leads us to ask, "What is the New English, if there is one?" This book is Professor Chisholm's answer to both questions. He believes that there is a New English, and he tells us wherein the newness lies.

For many years English as a school subject, like Caesar's Gaul, was divided into three parts: language, literature, and composition. It was a disjointed concept which all too often led to fragmentation in teaching and uncertainty in learning. "In a New English classroom," the author tells us, "language is the name of the game." In short, the newness here lies not so much in the discovery or adoption of a new body of content as in recognizing that all English activities are language-centered. Composition is essentially the use and manipulation of language. Literature consists of language used in special and formalized ways, for special purposes. One might even go so far as to insist that language is more than just the name of the game, it is the game itself.

At all events, it is in terms of this concept that the author proceeds, with initial attention to the new points of view, the ways of studying, analyzing and describing language which have developed over the past forty or fifty years. This in itself is an important contribution because at best the general public has only the foggiest notion about the discipline of linguistics. Here we find a lucid account of what interests the linguist and how he goes about his work, the classifications and terminology which have developed.

We proceed from the linguistic core to the various ways in which the pupil encounters and employs language — reading the printed page, studying literature, expressing himself in speech and writing. The author is a realist. He knows what goes on in countless classrooms: the innocuous theme assignments, the arid, encyclopedic approach to this novel or that play, the naïve commitment to this panacea or that for the teaching of reading.

At the same time he has an enlightened and informed view of what might come out of the school program in English. He is sensible on the issue of national goals, an issue which has been agitating educators ever since the conception of the National Assessment Program. "National goals do not presuppose a national program in the sense that every fifteen-year-old is reading the same book on the same day," he tells us. He has, moreover, an informed and sensitive conception of the linguistic needs and achievements demanded by a functioning democracy. "Tracking is neither all good nor all bad. It is probably more bad than good, though," "A young Negro who has to have Langston Hughes explained to him by a white man is not a 'slow learner.' He is a deprived learner. His agony has had no opportunity to be touched by a Negro poet."

In the light of such a concept of broad national need, we are led to see that reading is far more than being able to pronounce the words on a page. It is *knowing* what a sentence says, again a matter clearly beyond the dictionary definition of every individual word.

He sees the teaching of literature primarily as the development of sensitivity. As the foregoing paragraph but one suggests, there must be involvement and response, which demands a careful choice of literary selections to which response is possible, that students may come to know the pertinence, the ways, and the delights of literature.

What Professor Chisholm has to say about the teaching of composition will come as a shock to many. "A narrow, authoritarian view of correctness has nothing to do with good writing." "Ten thousand hours' drill on topic sentences, paragraphing, development, rhetorical lily gilding, and all the rest are ten thousand hours wasted if the student has no topic." "The weekly or monthly composition is a menace of the highest order. Children should write only when they want to"—namely, when they have something to say and feel that they must say it. This is strong medicine, but logically treated and forcefully presented.

All told, we have here a vigorously written account of the New English, making its points with simple, down-to-earth illustrations. As such, as a treatment of what is happening in the one school subject which engages the pupil's attention from the time he enters kindergarten until his graduation from high school, the subject upon which in his early school years he spends approximately half his time, it merits the attention and interest of parents, school board members, teachers, administrators—anyone in fact who is seriously concerned about the importance of language to our society, its function and operation in our society, and the value for the individual of mastering it, achieving a competence in it.

ALBERT H. MARCKWARDT
Princeton University

THE
NEW ENGLISH

1 | PRELIMINARIES AND BACKGROUND

It should be explained first what is meant by *The New English*. It is the emerging patterns of instruction in English in our schools. It is fresh emphasis on language based largely on the significant investigations of language that have been going on during the preceding two generations. It is an incorporation and a translation of these investigations and their results into the programs for instruction in English. It is an invigorated curriculum that looks less to rote learning, grammar drill, and stiffness of rhetoric than to basic understandings of language form and use. It encourages children and adolescents to ask provocative questions about literature and composition and to discover meaningful answers to their questions. Its goals are not dramatically different from those of previous generations, although means and techniques to achieve the desired ends are significantly different.

First, The New English leads students beyond literacy and competence to critical appreciation of all forms of communication, non-verbal as well as verbal. This means that whether the student is speaking, listening, writing, or reading he has the tools to weigh the success of the form and the content of the "message," whether it be from politician to audience, poet to listener, or student to parent.

Second, The New English provides students with keen insights into the workings of their own language and language in general. Heretofore, any knowledge gained of the structure and history of the English language was left largely to chance. These matters now are investigated forthrightly and in detail. The history of the English language is usually presented in high school although many grade school programs now cover this material. The structure of the language during earlier periods is commonly ascertained by using different versions of the same text from different periods. In this way the student grasps the idea that his language has a past, and his knowledge in turn suggests very strongly to him that the present varieties of the language are in the process of change. Recognition of this fact often leads positively to a lively curiosity about the nature and shape of this change.

Third, this New English generally frees the student to discover his own styles as speaker and writer of English. Freed from the drudgery of memorizing ancient "rules," he will enthusiastically embark upon the oldest and best learning of all—discovery.

With this much in mind it is now appropriate to turn to a brief account of English instruction in our tradition.

English has not always been a "subject" in school. In the Middle Ages, the place where the three "lower roads" of a liberal education met was, strictly speaking, the Commonplace. These three roads were *grammar, rhetoric,* and *logic.* Collectively, they were the *trivium.* (Something of the general disrespect in which they came to be held may be inferred from the present meaning of the word trivial.) The four upper division disciplines were mathematics, geometry, astronomy, and music. *Grammar* was largely a philosophical inquiry into spelling, sentences, "parts" of the sentence, and the like. *Rhetoric* was, and still is, the use of language, especially in the context of effective argumentation. Logic dealt then as now with the criteria of correct reasoning. Well through Shakespeare's time and on almost to the present, instruction in grammar, rhetoric, and logic continued in its essentially metaphysical vein with much emphasis on comparing, to almost everyone's chagrin, the vulgar English tongue to the noble, classical Greek, and in particular, to Latin. Literature, meanwhile, was a lesson in beauty and nobility. The great poets, many in translation from the same Greek and Latin, were studied, copied, and adored. Composition was formal and cold. One subscribed to the Master's rule or was rebuked most pitiously. One committed no grammatical "error," no logical blunder, no rhetorical *faux pas*. In sum, the privileged schoolboy was a perfect, if youthful, replica of his schoolmaster. His elocution was impeccable, his rhetoric faultless, and his grammar immaculate. Even so, he was a dull, opinionated snob who excelled in the trivial. I am speaking mostly of British lads of yore; however, their American counterparts, when they could be found in school, found themselves emasculated by a curriculum of "Good Manners" that bore no small resemblance to the English model. In any case, the study of rhetoric, grammar, literature, composition, and innumerable other matters fell ultimately and generally under the heading "English."

In some schools, the old or traditional English instruction which continues unaffected by accumulated knowledge is largely the ancient *trivium* in modern dress. To be sure, it is sometimes quite impossible to determine that the old is in command, what with multimillion-dollar "education plants," window walls, closed-circuit television, textbooks with current publication dates, and teachers whose skirt lengths are right up to the minute. But if the students shudder when the teacher announces a composition for next Friday, or if they weep when they get a B- on a spelling test, or if they may be overheard saying that they can't stand poetry, then we may be confident that the old ways are at work. These ways have always ~ tacitly assumed that there is a positive correlation between the study of "formal" grammar and competence in reading and composition, blithely unaware or unconcerned, certainly unpersuaded, that no such correlation exists. The fact is that hundreds and hundreds of investigations into the subject have proved faultlessly that there is no correlation between such matters. Such investigations, for example, have divided groups of students so that one group could be trained in formal grammar while the other group was given no training in grammar at all. At the end, each group was given a series of tests to determine how well they could write. *No significant difference was found in their respective abilities.* (A similar opinion concerning the correspondence between instruction in Latin grammar and competence in English grammar was widely held. But again, no such correspondence exists. Students who know Latin grammar are not significantly more knowledgeable of English grammar, nor can they "do better" with English grammar than students who have not studied Latin grammar.)

The old ways have coerced us into believing that "English" or "Language Arts" cannot be taught without textbooks, and that textbooks themselves must have pretty pictures in them, forgetting that the pictures that Homer's *Iliad* paints in the minds of children are worth infinitely more than all the Dick and Jane pictures in the world.

Of course, the most telling incrimination of the older modes of instruction may be seen by examining the results that they have had. The sad fact is that little more than literacy has been accomplished. Most of us who have managed to struggle our way through to high school graduation have come out readers and writers. But we have precious little understanding of how language is learned, of how our language functions, of how to interpret literature or speech without giving away the fact that we are enormous suckers for almost anybody's propaganda, or of how to write anything of any consequence. Most of us aren't sure whether "I saw him shoot her" is fact or opinion. We think it's time to buy a product when the advertiser says "All New—Just Out." We vote for the politician whom we're returning to office for the sixth successive time because he once again has told us that the first thing he is going to do is fix the roads. Never mind that nothing has been done to the roads in the past ten years. He belongs to the right party. It's a dreary, endless chronicle of the unfortunate results of well-intended instruction.

The messages that come to us by way of our eyes or our ears serve as stimuli for our own speech or action. Since our talk and our behavior are often inane or irresponsible or even dangerous, it may very well be that we have not been adequately prepared to deal intelligently and responsibly with these messages. One of the fond hopes for *The New English* is that a more responsible and vital citizenship will result from a frontal attack on what language is and how we use it.

During the 1930s and 1940s basic insights into language resulted from the codification of "linguistic science." In much the same way that the explosion of knowledge in other fields meant widespread change in curriculum, teacher-training, and instruction—for math, the sciences, and the social sciences—the explosion of knowledge of language, language learning, and language use has meant, first, a serious and fairly well-organized analysis of the methods and purposes of "English" instruction, and second, the emergence of new emphases, new techniques, and even new subject matter for that same instruction. For the first time it has become possible to teach English itself. Before now the content of English classes has been drama and the novel, philosophy, sociology, and morality, even sports and recreation. These were the matters that children studied, read about, and wrote about. But now, since we know a great deal about the English language *itself*, the content of English instruction can be broadened to include this first order of business. The internal form and variety of our own native language is now being taught. To borrow an insight from educational psychology, this new subject can be *learned* by our students. *They* ask the questions. *They* find useful answers.

It is true that when people talk or write they "encode messages" *about* philosophy, sociology, sports, or what have you. But people do so by manipulating purely linguistic forms—sounds, syllables, phrases—and these matters are now a subject in English classes. *How* do we talk or write about social subjects? What may be said about the noises we make or the letters we write quite apart from the meanings of the messages? ("We'll get to the meanings next!") These questions (and the answers that follow them) are immensely interesting to children. They are as fascinated by the microscopic world of language as they are the microscopic world of nature. Just as they want to know all about the stuff in the microscope—bacteria, blood cells, living organisms in a drop of water—so also they want to know about the basic building blocks of language. And the beauty part is that the biological world with its great variety and complexity is no more various and complex than the world of language. Here is a "subject," a content, that is perfectly apt in an English classroom. Here, in fact, is the true subject matter of English—English itself.

In recent years, the Modern Language Association and the National Council of Teachers of English have undertaken a loosely organized set of projects and investigations that have provided significant answers to the questions: *What are we to teach? How are we to teach it?* Similarly, university departments of English and Education and statewide associations of teachers of English have been participating in what has become a coordinated effort. "Project English" centers were set up all across the country some years ago, as were "curriculum centers" and variously named projects connected with the basic research and the ongoing investigations. The result has been, as should be clear by now, that a *New English* has blossomed, a plan that marries knowledge gained from studies and basic research to practical and intelligent goals for instruction in English. This little book is an introduction to this plan. The next chapter sets forth some of the more important things that are known about language along with some things that remain a secret. The succeeding chapters explain the science of language study and some of the results of this study as they relate to English, to the formulation of "new" grammars and how to teach them, and to the new techniques and aims in teaching literature, composition, and reading.

2 | LANGUAGE:
THE KNOWN AND THE UNKNOWN

Would you believe . . .

If man hadn't made language, there would be no chance of convincing anyone that it could be brought into being. But language is commonplace, and it is rather a shame that it is; the highest achievement of man following cognition—language—has gone almost unnoticed. Each man each day speaks thousands of words and hears many more, yet the monumental achievement of what he does escapes his notice. Even if a computer knew all the words of the English language and all its rules, it would take the computer billions of years to produce one given sentence. If we want to say "What's for supper?" we simply say it and think nothing of it. We select x number of sounds, put them in the right order, combine them in the right groupings, speak them with the appropriate "tune," or one of them—and think nothing of it. We could start writing down now *what happens* when someone says "What's for supper?" and never finish the job of recording all that the event includes. Thus, we can recognize not only that language is an invention of man but also that man has little appreciation of the workings of the thing he has made. In his daily use of language he is rarely consciously aware of the fact that the thing he is using is enormously complicated or that he is in near-perfect command of large portions of his language, saying whatever it is that is on his mind, interpreting whatever it is that someone says to him.

The Biology of Language

It is possible that "language" is over a million years old. It evolved in the course of man's development of his biological organs. In this sense, language is what the biologists call a "species specificity," a specialization that only humans have achieved. The organs of speech, of course, continue today to serve the biological functions of breathing (lungs, trachea, chest muscles, etc.), swallowing, and chewing. All languages are "produced" by managing these parts of the body in a highly specialized fashion. When we speak, the air is expelled from the lungs upward through the oral cavity, the nasal cavity, or both. Along the way we modify this air column in many ways: by giving it "voice" in the larynx, for instance, or by forcing it through a narrow slit formed at some point along its route (between the upper teeth and the tongue, for example, as in the formation of the first sound in the English word "thick").

Biologically speaking, language is probably not a primary attribute of the species; it serves no basic biological function. It has nothing to do *per se* with muscular coordination or respiration, even though without breathing and muscular activity there would be no language as we know it. At the same time, it is fairly clear that the actualization process that "realizes" language in individual men is innate. The processes through which languages are learned are deeply embedded in the species itself; in other words, these processes are rooted in man's biological nature.

As to the actual evolution of language in man, we can only make reasonable guesses concerning its rise and development. The primate biologist can delicately reassemble an earlier man from bits and pieces of him unearthed. If the skeletal remains go back far enough, say a million years, the "man" will be different in many particulars from modern man; that is, his bones will be different from ours. The differences are right before the biologist's eyes. But what is he to say of the language of the ancient man? He can only guess. That the

skull housed a brain that achieved "language" is a matter of specula-
tion. Cave drawings that evidence abstract thought are more reliable
indices of "language." Implements with symbolic legends on them
lend a greater credence to a "language-bearing man."

A primordial language similar to the highly structured systems we
know today (and by "today" I mean from now back in time a mere
five or ten thousands years) would be extremely unlikely. Language,
like other socio-cultural mechanisms, has evolved. There is evidence
that the "modern" linguistic feature of signaling meaning by com-
bining nonmeaningful sounds is a relatively recent development.
(When we say "man" we mean "male, adult, human," but it takes
two meaningless consonants and one meaningless vowel to say
"man." Presumably, somewhat earlier, *each* sound had meaning.)
Only recently did language evolve to the state where orderings of
individual sounds made for meanings.

Man belongs to the present geologic period—the Cenozoic, a
period in time running back only 60 million years. Sometime after
the formation of the western mountains in North America, but at
least 1.76 million years ago, man emerged as a distinct subspecies of
the *Hominoidea,* although so-called modern man is only 50,000 to
75,000 years old. He is a relative newcomer to the earth, since
plants, ferns, reptiles, scorpions, snails, sponges, and a host of
oldtimers have been around for well over 300 million years. In terms
of distance instead of time, if the universe were 100 miles long
instead of billions of years old, according to my calculations, we
would walk from the beginning of earth's time to within seventy-five
feet of the end of our one-hundred-mile trek before we would even
encounter man; and the last 4,000 years, man's recorded history,
would cover our last nine inches. We are a whippersnapper.

Man's language as we know it today with its intricate intra-
patterning cannot be much older than 50,000 years; a more likely
estimate would be 25,000 years. A number of arguments are ad-
duced in support of these figures. Cro-Magnon man evidenced signs
of socio-cultural systems, and it is unlikely that high social organization should develop without language, certainly not without communication. But unfortunately, even if the hypothesis could be
proved, it would in no way clarify what the communication system
was like. It may have been very complicated and still have been quite

different from the languages we know. Similarly, the argument that the "abstract" quality of cave drawings presupposes at least a "propensity" for language points to cognition in man, but cognition is not language.

In brief, some things are fairly clear about the biology and the evolution of language. But not very much is worth staking money on. The recent quickening of scientific interest in these matters will hopefully bring us some clearer understandings of "the biology of language."

Language is not writing.

Speech is not language, but neither is writing. It is obvious that printing, sign language, and non-verbal codes of different kinds are managed without the aid of lungs and oral cavity. However, these are not language. They are replicas or imitations of it, and like all imitations, they are in some sense "inferior." Not in the sense that a poem of Robert Frost's printed on a piece of paper is inferior to somebody's directions as to how to get to the laundromat, but in the sense that the printed poem fails to reproduce the oral act that *is* the poem, writing is inferior to language. It is in the sense that language precedes writing that language is understood as "superior" to writing.

From this point of view, it has become clear in recent times that the thing that should be understood first and best is language. Any understanding of writing or reading will follow from an understanding of speech and language. As we shall see later, this notion has had a significant impact on the teaching of English. In fact, it is probably this idea more than any other that has changed the direction of English instruction.

Language is symbolic.

It is true, then, that language is quite an achievement, that it is very old, that it is not, strictly speaking, biological, and that it is essentially oral. It is also symbolic. Words on a printed page—this page for example—are symbols for words that somebody might speak. (They are the words that I am saying to myself right now.)

But much more important than this, words that people speak are themselves symbols. The word spelled *m a n* is a symbol for the noises we make that constitute the word. This sequence of noises, in turn, is a symbol for the notion "man." It is a verbal symbol. When we say "Tom is my friend," we equate "Tom" with "friend." The one *is* the other. But the verbal act of saying "Tom is my friend" is an oral symbolizing of the agreement between "Tom" and "friend." "Tom" is a noise we make that verbally "stands for" (symbolizes) a human being. It is not our friend Tom. Tom is something else. He is a highly organized amalgam of living organisms. He may be in the same room with us when we say his name or he may be a thousand miles away. It makes no difference; nothing will happen to him in either case. Symbols don't act. They *are*. And it is clear that language is symbolic.

Language is an arbitrary convention.

Language is quite conventional, and in this sense, quite arbitrary, too. Any connection between what we say and non-language laws of various kinds is strictly coincidental. It is utterly arbitrary that the forms of a language should have arisen as they have. It is sometimes argued that in the beginning words were echoic, or that some of them were. "Ding," "meow," "hiss," and so forth no doubt evolved echoically, that is, by men making noises that imitated those they heard in nature. But no overall theory of the rise of natural languages attributes much to this phenomenon. If there were any laws governing such coinages, then all men would have agreed to the same noises. They didn't. English cats who say "meow" have a vowel sound at the end of what they say; French cats have an "1" sound. Furthermore, most words cannot be related at all to nature. None of the words in this sentence could conceivably be traced to extra-linguistic sources. It is a merely arbitrary, and subsequently conventional, agreement among generations of speakers that stands behind the emergence of forms in a language. This is not to say that there are no universals, no features of language that all languages share. There are. Selection and arrangement are two characteristics that all languages have in common. Indeed, one of the universals of language is this very element of arbitrary convention. Quite arbitrarily we have agreed to say what we do say (and *mean* what we say). But it should be noted that the agreement is not permanent. In other words, we agree to agree, but each day brings a new agreement. Those of us who have Anglo-Saxon forebears have ancestors who agreed to refer to pigs as "swine." They had no such word as "pig," which came along during the Middle Ages, and eventually, replaced the word "swine" in most contexts. A new agreement was thus "signed."

We see then that language is arbitrary in that the forms of individual languages arise without reference to any laws other than their own, but that having arisen, the speakers of the language conventionally abide by those same interior laws.

The authority of language

From this brief discussion, the arbitrary, conventional nature of language should be fairly clear. Of course, appeal to a higher authority than "speaker-agreement" is a favorite pastime for many of us. We feel more secure in the knowledge that somewhere in the stars it is written that such and such is the *right* form and such and such is the *wrong* form. "What's the correct way to say that?" we are fond of asking, not noticing that the question only arises over disputed forms. If there is no question in anybody's mind about how a word should be pronounced, then nobody gets excited. But if there is a question, then we are troubled. "What's the correct way to pronounce that? Shouldn't you really say two *r*'s in 'February'?" The idea behind the question is that somewhere there is an authority on this matter. It must be written down somewhere! But in language nothing is written down. In the case of "February" it may seem obvious that the authority for pronunciation is the spelling. "There are two *r*'s in 'February.' It should be pronounced with two *r*'s." But this authority is merely apparent; it is not real. There are very good historical and linguistic reasons for both one-*r* and two-*r* pronunciations. The word comes to us from Latin with two *r* letters and probably two *r* sounds. It stands the good chance of losing the first *r* sound by regular sound change. Meanwhile, the spelling with two *r*'s stays the same. The word "one" is pronounced one way and spelled another for the same reason: as the complicated set of changes in pronunciation proceeded, the spelling became fixed. Very few people would insist on a pronunciation of "one" that somehow followed the spelling. (I say few because I once received a letter from a man—a teacher of English, incidentally—who said it was high time we drove from vulgar mouths the *d*-less, two-syllable pronunciation of "Wednesday." He wanted everybody to say "Wed-nez-day." He would have had a fit over my pronunciation of "Wednesday, "February, second." I not only "mispronounce" "Wednesday" and "February"; I have a *t*-sound at the end of "second"!)

I hope the main point is clear[There *is* an authority for the use of language—*the people.*]When the people don't agree, the expected ruckus ensues. People of a higher social status succeed in intimidating people below them on the social scale. Meanwhile, the people down the line harden their position, and the unfortunate result is a good example of the polarization that typifies our society. Somewhere along the line we have perverted the ideal of democracy.

Speakers of a language enter into agreements, and it is these agreements that count, nothing else, nothing more. We have agreed to pronounce "February" in a variety of ways—or at least most of us have—and that's all there is to it.

Have you ever seen a living thing that didn't change?

The agreements, as we have seen, are to wholly conventional things. In the course of time, the agreements are amended in various ways so that eventually many things get changed utterly. This is another known attribute of language—*change.* The English language is not very much like it was a thousand years ago. It will bear small resemblance to its present state a thousand years from now.

Language is a living thing in the sense of the phrase that contrasts with such remarks as "Latin is a dead language." What we mean is that no one speaks Latin anymore. Many millions of people speak English, however. It is alive, and this means that it is subject to change. Change, for example, in vocabulary. All of the following are examples of vocabulary changes of various kinds: *psychedelic, Watusi* (the dance), *mod, laser, cinerama, sputnik, astronaut, Viet Cong, shoot* (the launching of a spacecraft), *television, escalation* (the heightening of the scale of war), *sit-in, love-in, walk-in, wade-in, team-teach, talkathon, highrise.* These are all newcomers. Vocabulary change also results in loss. *Chemise, gobbet, midwife, parasol, pursy, songbird* (female singer), and *toilette* are doomed if not already dead, consigned to books.

All aspects of language are subject to change, including the way words are arranged in sentences (*syntax*), the way words are changed internally (*morphology*), and the way words are pronounced (*phonology*). These things probably change rather more slowly than vocabulary, although it is difficult to be certain, because vocabulary change is more apparent than other kinds. Still, extensive change in any of these areas is a slow process. Six hundred years ago, *all* English words that had vowels in them that sounded like the letter *e* now have vowels that sound like the letter *i.* This means that *wine, ride, time,* and *I* sounded like *ween, reed, teem,* and *ee* in Chaucer's-day. The change took two or three hundred years to be completed. But change it did. And change language must.

Learning language

Much change is occasioned by the fact that children learn their language "imperfectly" from their parents. The discussion which ensues will owe much to the basic research that Eric Lenneberg has published. See especially his book *Biological Foundations of Language.* No individual has ever grown up speaking exactly the same language as his parents. He begins his overt language behavior mostly by imitating what he hears his parent say. But this imitative process hardly explains much about how language is learned. "Bye-bye," "doing?" "baby," "dada," "bottle," and so forth are a few of the words that English-speaking children "learn" at a very early age. The simple stimulus of the parent word results in the imitative response in the child. The parent says *"doggie"* many times, and the child imitates this noise and produces "gawk" or "gawkie" or "dawk" or "awg" or "goggie" or, in the case of a child on our block, "goggums" or some such word. Over time, he will learn to say "doggie" and "dog," or he will come very close to reproducing exactly what his parents have said. But there will be little differences here and there. His version might sound more like "dahg" than "dawg." The little differences, multiplied by millions of words and millions of children and enhanced by differences that result from separate sources, are the very substance of language change. So it is that change is understood as an attribute of all languages.

But we are dealing here specifically with language learning, not with some of its results. We can observe the language behavior of children directly and we can describe it very closely, but such a description says little about *how* the child is learning his language. It is obvious that in part the learning is imitative. We stop explaining what children do as imitative, however, when we observe them producing and understanding sentences that they have never heard before.

No mother or father needs to be reminded that the first verbal activity children engage in is crying. Gurgling, cooing, and squealing are fairly well-established by the time a child is three months old. All of these activities are essentially vowel-like in character. But interestingly enough, the "tune" of English is already being modulated in accordance with the parent language system. After six months, at least three English vowels and several consonants are being tried out in consonant-vowel syllables like "mu," "ba," "di," and the like. Many of the syllables produced do not sound much like English syllables (they sound more like Greek).

By the time the child is a year old he understands a few sentences ("Where's baby's nose?"), patterns of stress and pitch are becoming distinct, "sound play" is a favorite pastime, and "mama," "dada," and "bye-bye" are in his word repertory. After two years he has a vocabulary of more than fifty words, he speaks two- and three-word sentences ("Go home now," "Find Tommy," "Eat now," "My truck"), and most significantly, the child is interested for the first time in communicating information, and his interest in language *per se* is sharply on the increase. By the time he's three or four his vocabulary runs to more than a thousand words, a good deal of English syntax has been mastered, and the complicated business of getting the pitches and stresses right has become, if you'll pardon the expression, child's play. But again, the really wondrous thing is that most of his sentences are new ones to the language. He makes them up as he goes along. It is this feat that stumps us. How is it to be explained?

A child with a vocabulary of a mere dozen words could, mathematically speaking, produce over 479 million different sentences using all twelve words in different combinations each time. The number of possible combinations is incredibly higher if not all twelve are used necessarily for any one arrangement. It is true that a young American whose vocabulary includes "mama," "dada," "bottle," "bye-bye," "truck," "dolly," "go," "see," and three or four other words will not produce a sentence with all these words in it, nor will he, in fact, produce a sentence like "See bye-bye," or "Bottle my." This means that sentences are not merely mathematically possible combinations of words. There are factors at work which prevent certain *possible* arrangements. Still, children think up sentences that they have never heard before. Very young children do!

It is the process of acquiring the knowledge that permits this kind of linguistic performance that remains infuriatingly unknown. Neither the capacity nor the knowledge is directly observable. The "chemistry" of this capacity is only dimly understood. With language performance we can only surmise what must be the case concerning the knowledge we acquire that enables us to construct novel sentences and to interpret novel sentences that we hear. A theory of language learning that even feebly approximates how language is learned would be welcome. A theory that powerfully relates the observable to the source conditions, processes, and mechanisms of language acquisition would be truly valuable. Such a theory is being worked out at the present time, and we will take a close look at it in Chapter Four. For the present we can observe in this discussion of the known and the unknown of language that the *how* of language learning is a pretty deep mystery.

We conclude the discussion on language learning with a facet of it that is well-understood. Following the preliminary stage of "noise making" the child confronts *all* the attributes of language simultaneously. He learns words, pronunciations, meanings, and syntax (putting things together) all at once, not separately. He does not learn the sound system, then the word system, then the sentence system, then the "paragraph" system. It is true that babies speak very few sounds, fewer words, and no sentences. It is also true that children four or five years old speak zillions of sentences. But language learning is best considered as an upward spiraling, not a "first-this-then-that" kind of affair. In all events, it is learned. We are not born with it. We are probably born with a "trigger" which, once pressed, sets things at the ready for language learning.

Language has system.

If we learn language systematically, that is, by tackling everything at once, the thing we learn is itself systematic. If this were not so, no one would ever say anything to anyone and be understood. We have confidence that most of the agreements we entered into yesterday will hold for today. The child learns to depend upon "bye-bye" meaning the same thing from day to day. In this sense, language is viewed as neither anarchic nor chaotic. It has rules. It has system. The number of rules is far greater than all the grains of sand on all the beaches of the world. However many there are, we all subscribe to them. If there weren't any rules (patterned system), or if we could break them all at once, then language would cease to exist.

The rules I am speaking of are not of the kind: *Never say "can" when "may" is meant! Always begin a sentence with a capital letter!* No, the rules I am talking about are the ones that I am subscribing to in putting the words of this sentence in the right order. The rules I am talking about guarantee that when I say "What's for supper?" I will not be understood as having said "My hat is red" or even "What's for lunch?" I can fully expect an answer from someone concerning what will be eaten for the last meal of the day. (The next to last around our house. It's snacks at midnight for us.) These rules prohibit someone from saying "Yes" in answer to my question. They permit "Hamburgers" or "What do you feel like?" or a shrug, but not "Yes" or "Around six o'clock."

The rules, the system, are to be found everywhere—in the sounds we make, in the ways we put them together in syllables, in the words, their meanings, their phrasings, and even in the correspondence between these matters collectively and the culture that supports them.

The sounds of English are patterned and systematic. We begin syllables with almost any vowel or consonant sound (*up, on, apple, pass, mash, cat*). If we begin with a vowel sound, the next sound cannot be another vowel in the same syllable. If we begin with one of just a few consonant sounds (*f, b, t, g, d)*, we may proceed directly to certain other consonants, but only these. Words like *friend, blond, track, grind,* and *glad* illustrate these systematic features. At the ends of syllables we may find a single vowel sound *(sofa)* or a single consonant *(track)*. There may be two consonant sounds, three, even four (*worlds*), but no more. In two-member consonant clusters at the ends of syllables, we may have *-st* (*last*) or *-ts (hats), -nd (sand)* but not *-dn.* We have *-fs (cuffs)* but not *-vs, -pt (stopped)* but not *-tp.* And so on and so on. All strictly patterned and systematic.

In like fashion, there is system and pattern at every turn among words and their meanings. As we have seen, we rely on the relative stability of the word meanings themselves. *Supper* does not mean *lunch.* But we also have confidence in all our morphological processes remaining constant. *Friendliness* we recognize as a word, but not *friendnessly.* We know that if we want to talk about more than one *hat* we are obliged to "add something onto the end," namely *-s.* The *-s* doesn't go in the middle or at the beginning, and it isn't anything other than *-s.* Needless to say, this kind of thing is so complicated and so immense in scope that it would take many books to contain it all. Still, notice something extremely important, please. *We have it all in our heads!*

As for syntax, what would happen if we couldn't depend on "subjects" *doing things* to "objects"? Suppose we woke up one day to discover that sometimes "The man chased a woman" meant "The man chased a woman" but other times it meant "A woman chased the man." How awful! We have enough trouble communicating as it is without throwing over this fundamental syntactic property of English sentences. We depend on it. We depend on syntax being *systematic.*

In summary, then, we say that language is one marvelous "invention," but it is more social than biological. It is verbal, symbolic, arbitrary, conventional, living, changing, "learned," systematic, and patterned. That's a lot. It is also, upon occasion, propagandistic, poetic, instructive, prosaic, eloquent, dull, stirring, or combinations of these things. Any English program, certainly The New English program, should devote itself to these aspects of language; in fact, we say seriously that the *uses* of language are the principal concerns of instruction. But it should be stressed that a right understanding of the uses of language follows from an understanding of language itself. The right understanding of language results from a study of what is demonstrably true of "patterned vocal behavior." Such a study undertaken over a period of years is at the very heart of The New English. One of the ways of studying language, and some of the results of the study, as they relate to English, are the topics of the next chapter.

3 | THE STRUCTURE OF ENGLISH

Structural linguistics

Structural linguistics refers to that social science whose business it is to discover how a particular language works. It has a complicated early history, but for the purposes of this discussion, structural linguistics may be said to have begun in our country with the publication of two books, Edward Sapir's *Language: An Introduction to the Study of Speech,* and Leonard Bloomfield's *Language.* Without these two books, there almost certainly would have been no New English.

Bloomfield and Sapir laid stress on the fact that speech was the primary subject for investigation. Both felt that the system of articulated speech sounds that people use to carry on their affairs was the thing to be analyzed. Their work with American Indian languages and the principles they discovered for such work became the foundation for subsequent studies. The effect that Bloomfield has had on the teaching of English has been the greater, since it was he who insisted that definitions be based on the forms in the languages, not on any particular model or tradition. Bloomfield's work on Indian languages led him into a world where few grammarians before him had ventured. He "discovered" categories of structure in these languages that defied any traditional treatment; and he found that some sacred cows of latinate, or classical, grammar had no relevance to the structure of this or that Indian language, or, more to the point, to the English language. Furthermore, he found that there was no such thing as a primitive language. He found, true enough, many languages that were being spoken by the members of "primitive" societies. But he did not find any language to be "simple" or "unstructured." They were all very old, very complicated languages, each perfectly suited to the linguistic-cultural needs of the people who used them. Sound systems, word systems, and syntactic systems all were found to be of long standing and high complexity. No two languages were discovered to be identical or even nearly so. Grammatical categories in one language had no counterpart in another. And so on.

All of this led Bloomfield and other early researchers to conclude that a way had to be found to analyze languages other than by superimposing Latin grammar on them. This new way came to be known as *structural linguistics,* sometimes called *descriptive linguistics.* This new way looked only at verbal behavior. It presumed nothing about the structure of the language before it got going on the analysis.

Structural linguistics is a science. But it is not a pure science like chemistry. It is a social science like psychology for a good and obvious reason: languages are made and used by men. Except when man is "talking to himself," he is engaging in a social activity whenever he speaks. He asks questions so that he may learn. He makes statements so that he may be understood. Thus, any investigation into his overt verbal behavior becomes a social investigation.

Now recognition of the social nature of the investigation means that the world of pure science is not possible for structural linguistics. The chemist deals with a world that man has not produced. The chemical composition of table salt is something over which man has no control. It is there unsullied in the chemist's lab awaiting his analysis. He can lay it bare before his eyes so that he can say of what it is made, segment, and classify it to his heart's content. He can say "sodium, chlorine, chemical bond, nucleus, proton, molecule." He can say all that can demonstrably and verifiably be said about table salt. The structural linguist, however, is not so fortunate. He cannot do the same thing to speech. For thirty years after Bloomfield he tried to, but many of the techniques of the pure scientist were modified along the way. In the first place, the laboratory of the linguist looks not at all like that of a pure scientist, of our chemist, for example. No Bunsen burners, no pipettes, no beautiful bottles with colorless dynamite in them. The structural linguist's lab is a place for two, a place for himself and the speaker of a language. Instead of glass and hardware of limitless variety, his tools are a pad, a pencil, and occasionally a tape recorder.

The chemist can take his sweet time analyzing his table salt. It will not die out in the air as speech does. But the linguist cannot dawdle. Language does not exist in a bottle; it is there one minute, gone the next. He must catch it, as it were, on the wing, using whatever equipment he finds is satisfactory to "catch" speech—pad, pencil, tape recorder, and, as we shall see, a very special alphabet.

In one way or another, the linguist gets his "informant" to speak. He holds objects up, he acts things out, he points to things, and all the while, he *writes down* what the informant says. For his purposes, obviously, he cannot use the English alphabet to record a natural language. He must use a special alphabet that will enable him to write down exactly what is said, an alphabet with a one-to-one correspondence to the varieties of speech sounds that speakers of languages use. In the case of English, for example, there must be one symbol for the first consonant sound in *they* and a different symbol for the first sound in *thick*. In English writing, we spell these two different sounds with the same sequence of letters, *th*. But one sound is *voiced*, the first sound of *they*, while the other is *voiceless* (as in whispering), the first sound of *thick*. It wouldn't do for the linguist to write down two different sounds with the same symbol. That would be like a chemist using the same symbol to refer to two different chemicals.

The International Phonetic Alphabet (IPA) proved to be the most suitable for the job the linguist had in mind. In this alphabet there are seven or eight dozen basic symbols, each one used to represent a very carefully defined sound. There are also several *diacritical marks* that are used to give specialization designations to the individual base symbols. Together, these devices enable the linguist to record the close phonetic detail of the sounds his informant makes. He must be able to make fine distinctions with his alphabet because, in the early stages of his analysis, he does not know which differences between sounds matter and which do not. For all he knows, since he assumes nothing, the phonetic difference between the first sounds of *they* and *think* may not matter in the sound system of English. But he doesn't know, so he writes down the difference. If he does not do his work meticulously, the written record of the informant's speech will be inaccurate, and the analysis of the language will be faulty.

Suppose, for example, that the linguist failed to record the distinction in English between the vowel sounds of *ten* and *tin*. You may say that this is incredible, that they are obviously different. But that is only because the difference "counts" in English, and for mature speakers of English, recognizing what counts is easier than falling off a very round log. But the *physical* difference between the two sounds is really extremely small. If you sound just the middle of the two words, that is, just the vowels, you will notice that the change from the vowel sound of *ten* to that of *tin* is a matter of raising the jaw and the tongue a trifle. Here we have a small—but very significant—difference. This is what phonological analysis is all about: small but significant differences among sounds.

It is quite possible for the linguist to detect different pronunciations of the word *ten*. As a matter of fact, it isn't possible to say the word the same way twice. For example, on one occasion we may say the word relatively quickly, as in *ten of them,* and on another occasion we may say it relatively slowly: *eight . . . nine . . . ten.* The vowels will be fast and slow, too. That is, they will be *physically different.* But does this particular physical difference matter? Linguists have discovered, however, that the physical difference between the vowel sounds in *ten* and *tin* does matter—it is phonemic—whereas the physical difference between the vowels in fast and slow *tens* doesn't matter—it is not phonemic. That's about all there is to it.

Sooner or later, usually sooner, the linguist sets about to describe the structure of the language that he has elicited from his informant. The analysis is presented under the following headings: *phonology, morphology,* and *syntax. Phonology* has to do with what we have just been talking about, the sound system. *Morphology* deals in word-forming elements and words themselves, whether simple or complex. And *syntax* deals with the interrelationships among words in a sentence.

The phonological structure of someone's speech is explained in terms of what we have called *phonemes*. These are the sound units of a language. The system of phonemic units is an interlocking network of sound contrasts. In other words, all the possible pronunciations of the middle part of *ten* are in phonemic contrast with all those of *tin*—and with all those of *ton*—and with those of *tan, tune,* and *tone.* Technically again, *any group of phonetically similar sounds that forms a significant set of contrasts with any other group of phonetically similar sounds is a phoneme.*

Here's a simple illustration. Say the two short sentences below out loud.

> He spelled it.
> He spilled it.

There is only one small but significant difference between these two sentences. (It's the same difference that we had between *ten* and *tin*.) The vowel in the middle of *spelled* is phonemically different from the vowel in *spilled*. We write the vowel phoneme in *spelled* between slant lines, /e/, and that of spilled, /i/, to distinguish the writing from English writing. You might like to see how these two words are "spelled" phonemically: /speld/ and /spild/. *Spoiled*, incidentally, would be /spoyld/, but we'll see much more of this a little later on.

Now, let's get technical for one more minute. Phonemes have *allophones.* These are the things that we say, since it is obvious that you can't say groups of sounds as a single sound. Consider the *p* phoneme in English, /p/. There are two allophones for this phoneme, two different *p* sounds. One of them is the *p* sound at the beginning of *pin.* If you say it out loud with your hand in front of your mouth, you will feel a little puff of breath bounce off your palm. This puffed *p* is called an *aspirated p.* The *p* of *spin* is different physically. It has no puff of breath. It is *unaspirated.* That's two different *p* sounds. And that's two allophones for the /p/. (The kids came home yesterday talking about universal sets, unions, and intersections. Today, they are coming home talking about phonemes and allophones.)

When the linguist has sorted out what counts and what doesn't on the phonological level, that is, after he has identified all the phonemes and their allophones, he turns his attention to combinations of phonemes that are repeated over and over again in the record of his informant's speech. These combinations must have some kind of meaning. And this meaning must be found in the smallest possible combinations. These too he has a fancy name for; *morpheme, the unit of form.* If he has recorded the speech of his informant long enough, he has, for English let's say, numerous instances of *ten,* or /ten/. Each time it has been the same three phonemes in the same order. /ten/ repeats in the speech of the informant over and over again with the same meaning. Voila! a *morpheme.* You can see where this leads: to a practically limitless listing of such forms.

It must be stressed that morphemes are units of minimal meaning—*any kind of meaning.* How many morphemes do you suppose are in the following little sentence?

The dogs seem friendly.

Very good! Six is right. Let's mark them off.

The| dog|s |seem |friend |ly.

The means "the." *Dog* means "dog." *-s* means "plural." *Seem* means "seem." *Friend* means "friend." And *-ly* means "like." You see, morphemes are *not* words.

Each morpheme in a language has at least one *morph.* Allomorphs are the phonemic forms that morphemes take. For *dog* there is only one morph. So also for *friend.* But for "*plural*" there are many. There's /z/ at the end of *dogs.* There's /s/ at the end of *cats.* And there's /əz/ at the end of *bushes.* These three different phonemic elements—/z/, /s/, and /əz/—are the *same* morphemically.

Once all of the morphemes of a language have been identified, they must be classified. In English, great numbers of morphemes are *free forms,* that is, they occur in isolation, independently. *Ten* is such a form, written {*ten.*}So are {*dog*}, {*cat*}, {*pin*}, {*spin*}, and thousands of other such forms. Not all free forms are free morphemes, though. *Cats,* for example, is a free form that consists of two morphemes, {cat} and {*plural* }. {Cat}is a free morpheme. {*plural* }is a *bound* morpheme. Bound morphemes never occur freely. They are always tacked onto something.

Bound morphemes may be further classified. Some of them are *derivational* and some are *inflectional.* Inflectional morphemes can only come last in a series of two or more morphemes that make up a free form. {*plural*} is one of these. This makes the -*s* part of *cats* an inflectional morpheme. But the -*y* part of *catty* is a derivational morpheme. And so is the -*ness* part of *cattiness*.

In sum, free forms consist of one or more morphemes. Some free forms consist of a single free morpheme: {*pin*}, {*spin*}, etc. Some others consist of free and bound forms in combination. Words are made up of morphemes, which in turn are made up of phonemes. Bound morphemes are either derivational or inflectional.

But that's enough technical terminology for a while.

The inventory of morphemes in a language is something more than a listing. It is a classification that is a window through which we can see the dim outline of some of the mysteries of the internal structure and form of the language. In this, structural linguistics behaves respectably, classification being the bread and meat of science.

No such for morphemes.

Next, syntax. It isn't until we get here that we are able to make the most interesting and significant classification of any large group of morphemes or combinations of morphemes. English sentences are strings of morphemes that may be shown to have certain *privileges of occurrence.* Take *My dog ran away,* for example. Considering the morphemes in this sentence, it may fairly be observed that no other combination of them is possible. We must say *My dog ran away,* not **Dog my ran way a-.* The word *my* has the privilege of occurring before *dog* and only there; *ran* comes after *dog,* and so forth. Now consider

> His dog ran away.
> Her dog ran away.
> That dog ran away.

as well as

> My cat ran away.
> My friend ran away.
> My uncle ran away.

Such sentences reveal that certain forms distribute themselves in the same way over and over again. (Here's *same* again.) We can say of such words that they form a class *on the basis of this observable*

---

*The asterisk is used here and elsewhere to mark a phrase that would be rejected as nongrammatical by the speakers of a language.

behavior. They form a *distributional* class because *his, her, my, that* and so forth share some stated behavioral habit. Similarly, *dog, cat, friend, uncle,* and so forth make up another class of word because they share a different distributional behavior.

Following this same general principle of looking for patterns of form, classification may be conducted by recognizing inflectional-derivational features. Usually, distributionally identified classes are simultaneous with inflectionally or derivationally derived classes. As it happens, *dog, cat,* etc. not only distribute themselves in sentences in ways that are peculiar to themselves syntactically, but they also inflect in ways that no other group of words does. Everybody knows that *dog, cat,* etc. inflect for the plural: *dogs, cats,* etc. The structural linguist especially knows this, and knowing it, he says that the words form an inflectional class. *All* words that inflect for the plural belong to the same class.

This is word classification. Syntax itself studies the relationships that words enter into phrases, clauses, and sentences. It is a very complicated study. Suffice it to say here, as we are developing an overview of structural linguistics, that English syntax involves the investigator in an analysis of the structures of prediction, conjunction, modification, complementation, and other wondrous things.

Let's consider just one of these processes to see what syntax *feels* like. Consider structures of *modification.* This is not the old stuff and nonsense about "an adjective is a word that modifies the meaning of a noun." Since there is no way in the universe to test such a "definition" objectively, there is no way to make it work. We could say that any old word in any old sentence is an adjective simply by stomping our feet and yelling "Oh yes, it *does* modify that noun!" But there can be none of this in a scientific grammar.

In the modification we are talking about here, we are referring, at one point at least, to what *my* and *little* are doing in *my little pussycat.* We are referring to *noun phrases* and *satellites* and *heads* and other objectively arrived-at categories of grammar. Look at this list of English phrases.

my little pussycat
both the boys
no single entry
the first method
these quiet streets
jazz trombones

Each has an indispensable part, the head. This part comes last. The satellites come before the head. If there is more than one satellite, the order of them follows rules governing their arrangement. It is the business of the syntactician to discover all the rules for all the arrangements for all the different kinds of word groupings that a language has. After all the rules are written, syntax is finished, and the structural grammar is "complete."

The linguist has his techniques of segmentation and classification based on the identification of patterns of form that repeat in a language. If these modes of analysis result in statements that other grammars or other grammarians are familiar with and which they approve, or if they do not, the linguist keeps his cool. All he cares about is that his statements, like those of his chemist friend, follow from scientifically valid analytical procedures and that they therefore be vulnerable to proof.

The Structure of English

Modern American English has nine vowel phonemes, four semi-vowel phonemes, twenty consonant phonemes, and twelve intonational phonemes. That's a total of forty-five: a network of forty-five sound-unit contrasts.

	Front	Center	Back	
High u	i	ɨ	u	r
n				o
r				u
o				n
Mid u	e	ə	o	d
n				e
d				d
e				
Low d	æ	a	ɔ	

The nine vowel phonemes are sketched in the graph above. Reading from the left across the top, we have: /i/ in *pin,* /ɨ/ in unstressed syllables of numerous words, /u/ in *look.* In the middle row, from left to right, we have: /e/ in *said,* /ə/ in *cup* or in the second syllable of *sofa*, /o/ in *obey*. In the bottom row, again left to right, there are: /æ/ in *cat*, /a/ in *pot*, and /ɔ/ in *caught*. Thus:

/i/	*six, women, fear*
/ɨ/	*just (unstressed)*
/u/	*look, woman, tour*
/e/	*mess, against, care*
/ə/	*cup, roses, sofa*
/o/	*obey, store*
/æ/	*cat, land, plaid*
/a/	*pot, palm, farm*
/ɔ/	*caught, law*

(A person who does not distinguish between *cot* and *caught* will be perplexed by these "key words." They are meant merely to suggest the contrasts that are typical in English.)

The designations on the graph refer to relative tongue positions. /i/, /ɨ/, and /u/ are pronounced with the tongue held higher in the mouth than for /e/, /ə/, and /o/. In turn, it is higher for /e/, /ə/, and /o/ than for /æ/, /a/, and /ɔ/. (If you pronounce *sit* then *sat*, you will notice that the tongue goes down for the vowel in *sat*.) Similarly, /i/, /e/ and /æ/ are pronounced with the tongue farther forward in the mouth than it is for /ɨ/, /ə/, and /a/. And again, the tongue is still farther back for /u/, /o/, and /ɔ/ than for /ɨ/ /ə/, and /a/. Finally, the lips are rounded for the back vowels /u/, /o/ and /ɔ/. They are not rounded for the front vowels.

The reader who has kept track of the vowel phonemes in the key-word listing will have noticed that the vowel sounds in *feel, fool, fail, foal, file, foul*, and *furl* are missing. That's because the nine vowels listed are "simple" vowels. They are what are called *monophthongs*. The vowel nuclei in *feel* and *fail* and the others are *diphthongs*. When we say *fail* and *file*, we start at one place for the vowel and slide to another. The tongue rises and goes forward in the mouth in both cases. In the same way, when we say *foul* and *foal*, the tongue rises, but this time goes back. In both cases, it starts one place and goes to another. (That makes a diphthongal sound. The first part of a diphthong is called the *on-glide*, the second part, the *off-glide*.) The off-glide in *fail, feel, file*, and *foil* is a semivowel, and it is written phonemically /y/. The off-glide in *fool, foal*, and *foul* is also a semivowel, and it is written /w/. Finally, the off-glide in *furl* is written /r/. All of this may be expediently summarized as follows:

feel	/fiyl/
fool	/fuwl/
fail	/feyl/
foal	/fowl/
file	/fayl/
foul	/fawl/
foil	/foyl/
furl	/fərl/

The fourth semivowel is /h/.

The twenty consonant phonemes are usually displayed according to series and order, as follows:

	Bi-labial	Labio-dental	Dental	Alveolar	Palatal	Velar
voiceless PLOSIVES	/p/			/t/	/k/	
voiced	/b/			/d/	/g/	
voiceless FRICATIVES		/f/	/θ/	/s/	/š/	
voiced		/v/	/ð/	/z/	/ž/	
voiceless AFFRICATES				/č/		
voiced				/ǰ/		
LATERALS				/l/		
NASALS	/m/			/n/		/ŋ/

Bilabial	means "both lips."
Labiodental	means "one lip and one row of teeth," ("the uppers").
Dental	means that same row of teeth.

Alveolar   means the part of the mouth just back
of the upper teeth.

Palatal   means the "hard palate."

Velar   means the "soft palate," the velum.

Plosive   means "explosive" sound.

Fricative   means "with friction."

Affricate   means partly plosive and partly fricative.

Lateral   means "around the sides of the tongue."

The six plosives /p/, /t/, /k/, /b/, /d/, and /g/ are consonant phonemes that occur as the first sounds in *pill, till, kill, bill, dill, and gill* respectively. But here are some more key words that illustrate the distribution of the phonemes.

/p/   *pill, spill, paper, lips*

/t/   *till, still, eight, washed*

/k/   *kill, skill, racket, quaint, lick, ache*

/b/   *bill, rubber, cab*

/d/   *dill, bottle, rudder, moved*

/g/   *gill, juggler, guard, rugs*

The eight fricatives /f/, /v/, /θ/, /ð/, /s/, /z/, /š/, and /ž/, occur as the first sounds in *fairy, very, thin, then, Sue, zoo, shun,* and *Jules* (with a French pronunciation), respectively. /ž/ doesn't occur first in any English word. It occurs at the end of *rouge* and in the middle of *azure*, however. This phoneme is our newest consonant, incidentally. It's only five hundred years old.

/f/   *fairy, affair, life, tough*

/v/   *very, over, of*

/θ/   *thin, ether, wreath*

/ð/   *then, either, breathe*

/s/   *Sue, duster, mice, moss*

/z/   *zoo, presume, as*

/š/   *shun, nation, rash*

/ž/   *rouge, azure*

The two affricates /č/ and /ǰ/ occur as the first sounds in *chin* and *gin* respectively.

/č/   *chin, question, etch*

/ǰ/   *gin, magic, budge*

/l/ occurs as the first sound in *lap*, /m/ as the first sound in *map*, and /n/ as the first sound in *nap*. /ŋ/ is like /ž/ in that it never occurs first in any English word. It is the sound at the end of *song*, or the one before /g/ in *finger*.

/l/   lap, sloppy, alloy, help, ball
/m/   map, small, rimmed, limb
/n/   nap, knot, sand, plan
/ŋ/   song, finger, snapping

The twelve intonational phonemes (some people count eleven) are rather more difficult to describe, but let us try, first, by observing that English is not spoken in a monotone. When we say that someone speaks in a monotone we probably mean that his high pitches are not much higher than his lows. If his mid pitch is a C on the scale, then he rarely goes much higher than an E or lower than an A.

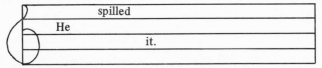

In normal English, though, there are highs, mids, and lows that are more dramatically different from one another. When most of us say *How are you?* we are pretty high on the *are* part, pretty low on the *you* part, and about mid-range for *how.*

These three "frequency vibration" contrasts are *pitch* phonemes. There is one other pitch phoneme, a very high one. All four are written phonemically with numbers, usually /1/, /2/, /3/, and /4/, from low to high:

/3/
/2/ How are you?/1/

Stress, or relative loudness, is a little easier. When we read monosyllables as from a list, each one receives about the same force of articulation. In a shopping list, for example,

soap
milk
bread
eggs
tea
fruit

each word gets about the same "push," or stress.

Some syllables are stressed more strongly than others, though, in a list like the following:

coffee
pickles
raisins
mustard
ketchup

Notice that each of these words has two syllables and that the first syllable of each word has a stronger stress than the second syllable. Now say

grapefruit
hamburger

Grapefruit is different stresswise than *coffee* or *ketchup*. The first syllable in *grapefruit* is strong, but the *-fruit* part of *grapefruit* is stronger than the *-ee* part of *coffee*. These facts give us three degrees of stress: there is the strong one on the first syllable of *coffee*, there is the weak one on the second syllable of *coffee*, and there is the one in between on the second syllable of *grapefruit*.

But there is a fourth degree of stress. Everyone who shops in supermarkets knows what a *check-out counter* is. It's the place where the grocer gets his, so to speak. But consider what we say when we say *check-out counter*, especially the *-out* part. It is weaker than both the *check-* part and the *count-* part. But it is stronger than the *-er* part. That makes four stresses. The whole phrase can now be marked with stress phonemes: /´/ is the strong one, called *primary stress;* /^/ is the next strongest, called *secondary stress;* /ˋ / is the third degree of stress, called *tertiary stress;* and /-/ is the weak one called, strangely, *weak stress.*

chéck-oùt coûntĕr

Students agree that *juncture* is the most difficult phonemic concept to grasp. Mostly, I think it is because here we are talking about *nothing,* for, you see, juncture is often mere silence. But everyone who tells dirty jokes to maiden aunts knows very well that silence can be quite meaningful. So it is. Silence is golden. It is also phonemic. If we count to four, whether fast or slow there are little pauses (silences) between certain of the phonemes in the stream of speech. These silences are essential. Without them, we would not only not be able to count to four and be understood, we wouldn't be able to say much of anything to anybody. When we count to four, as I have said, there are short pauses between *one* and *two* and between *two* and *three*, a slightly longer pause between *three* and *four*, and of course, a l o n g pause after *four*. That long pause is part of the signal for "the end." These pauses operate systematically in the language. They contrast with one another in the same ways that different consonant phonemes or different vowel phonemes do. In this case, then, the only difference between otherwise identical phrases is that one has one kind of juncture and the other has a different kind. Consider the difference between

Fine Dan.

Find Anne.

Not the spelling difference. Remember, that's just a *writing* convention. We are interested here in *speech* conventions. Each expression consists in the identical phonemic segments; /fayndæn/ shows the consonant and vowel phonemes; /2fayndǽn 1/ shows the pitches and the stresses. So far, they are indentical phonemically. But we know the two phrases are different! *Fine Dan* is not *Find Anne*. We know they are different because we speak them with *contrastive junctures*, namely,

Fine Dan   /2 faŷn + ^{3}dǽn 1/

Find Anne   /2 faŷned + ^{3}ǽn 1/

These junctures, as can be seen, are written /+/ and are called, believe it or not, *plus junctures*.

Once again we have revealed something about the way our language works that is buried so deep that it took hundreds of years for people to "discover" it. It has been there all the time, naturally, just as antimatter has been there all the time. But now it has been thresholded by the tools of a modern social science. As with other revelations, it merely provides man with a broader knowledge of the world he has made for himself. For this reason alone the search for such knowledge finds justification. But as we shall see in Chapter Four, it has a more practical reason for being in the classroom.

Back to more pedestrian matters, if only for a moment. Juncture, like pitch and stress, operates a four-way network of contrasts, which is to say that there are four junctures in English written in various ways, sometimes with arrows, sometimes with plusses and crosshatches, etc. One of the more fascinating of these is the juncture called *terminal*. It is an apt name—"the end." When we count to four; the voice level, having risen, falls all the way through four; the sounds of *four* are stretched out; there is a nice *l o n g* pause at the end. These things constitute terminal juncture. Doing all these things while saying *four* is like telling someone who is listening to the count, "Here's the end. I'm finished."

Try this once. Count to four in the usual way. "One, two, three, four." Now say "five."

One, two, three, four. Five.

If anybody is listening to you, he will think that you have lost your mind. You have given him the wrong signal. You "told" him by the way you counted to four that that was as far as you were going to count. Then you "finished again" with the extra number. Interesting!

There is a four-way network of junctural contrasts in English. We have seen one, /+/, which keeps *Fine Dan* and *Find Anne* apart (as well as *announce* and *an ounce* and a host of others), and another, terminal juncture, /#/, which marks off the ends of sentences. The other two we can pass over here very quickly by merely observing that they help us get around the sides of *Mr. Smith* in sentences like

My friend Mr. Smith is here.
My friend, Mr. Smith, is here.
My friend, Mr. Smith is here.

And with this observation, we have come to the end of the description of English phonemes. All together, as we said at the beginning, there are forty-five, that is, a network of forty-five sound-unit contrasts for modern American English, whatever dialect we happen to be talking about.

Here's a tabulation of the forty-five phonemes for ready reference.

Simple vowels   /i/, /ɨ/, /u/, /e/, /ə/, /o/, /æ/, /a/, /ɔ/

Consonants   /p/, /t/, /k/, /b/, /d/, /g/, /f/, /v/, /θ/, /ð/, /s/, /z/
                /š/, /ž/, /č/, /ǰ/, /l/, /m/, /n/, /ŋ/

Semivowels   /y/, /w/, /h/, /r/

Pitches   /1/, /2/, /3/, /4/

Stresses $/\acute{\ }/, /\text{-}/, /\grave{\ }/, /\check{\ }/$

Junctures $/+/, /|/, /\|/, /\#/,$ or $/+/, /\rightarrow/, /\downarrow/$

The morphological and morphemic structure of English is relatively uncomplicated; however, the immense detail involved prevents a full discussion in this presentation.

The morphemes of English divide roughly into three groups: *base morphemes, affixal morphemes* (things "attached"), and *intonational morphemes. Base morphemes* are the irreducible parts that serve as springboards for complex forms. Conversely, they are the things left over after everything else has been cut away. *Hat,* for example, is a base form. *Hatful* is not. Neither is *hatfuls.* Both are complex forms made up of base forms and affixal forms. The *-ful* and the *-s* are *affixal morphemes.* They are "attached." Since they are attached at the end, they are called suffixes. Sometimes affixal morphemes are attached at the beginning, as in *return, antiwar,* and *confer.* Such affixes are prefixed to the bases and are called prefixes.

Now let's see what some of this actually looks like in the patterned structure of English. Consider first the past-tense morpheme, {-d}. When we say *He spilled it,* the last sound of *spilled* tells us "past tense." The spilling is not happening now, it is not going to happen sometime in the future; it happened in past time. We write the morpheme as {-d} because usually the phoneme that occurs as this morpheme is /d/, as in the following:

> He spilled it.
> He rubbed it.
> He wagged it.
> He obeyed it.
> He fanned it.
> He mowed it.

Sometimes the past tense morpheme occurs as /t/, as in

> He brushed it.
> He faced it.
> He liked it.
> He dressed it.

and some others. Finally, some verb bases take /-əd/ as the past-tense sign:

> He sighted it.
> He edited it.

He batted it.

He graded it.

The occurrence of one or the other of these phonemic representations of the past-tense morpheme is largely predictable. If the base of the verb ends in /p/, /k/, /f/, /θ/, /s/, /š/ or /č/, the /-t/ allomorph of the {-d} morpheme will be suffixed to the base.

BASE	+	PAST TENSE	=	FULL FORM	
skip	/skip/	-ed	/t/	skipped	/skipt/
lick	/lik/	-ed	/t/	licked	/likt/
cough	/kɔf/	-ed	/t/	coughed	/kɔft/
berth	/bərθ/	-ed	/t/	berthed	/bərθt/
miss	/mis/	-ed	/t/	missed	/mist/
rush	/rəš/	-ed	/t/	rushed	/rəšt/
botch	/bač/	-ed	/t/	botched	/bačt/

If the base of the verb ends in /b/, /g/, /v/, /ð/, /z/, /ž/, /ǰ/, /r/, /l/, /m/, /n/, /ŋ/, /y/, or /w/, the allomorph /-d/ will be suffixed to the base.

BASE	+	PAST TENSE	=	FULL FORM	
rub	/rəb/	-ed	/d/	rubbed	/rəbd/
hug	/həg/	-ed	/d/	hugged	/həgd/
love	/ləv/	-ed	/d/	loved	/ləvd/
writhe	/rayð/	-ed	/d/	writhed	/rayðd/
razz	/ræz/	-ed	/d/	razzed	/ræzd/
rouge	/ruwž/	-ed	/d/	rouged	/ruwžd/
judge	/ǰeǰ/	-ed	/d/	judged	/ǰeǰd/
dare	/der/	-ed	/d/	dared	/derd/
pull	/pul/	-ed	/d/	pulled	/puld/
cram	/kræm/	-ed	/d/	crammed	/kræmd/
phone	/fown/	-ed	/d/	phoned	/fownd/
wing	/wiŋ/	-ed	/d/	winged	/wiŋd/
tree	/triy/	-ed	/d/	treed	/triyd/
stow	/stow/	-ed	/d/	stowed	/stowd/

And then, if the base of the verb ends in either /t/ or /d/, the /-əd/ allomorph is attached to the base to form the past tense.

BASE	+	PAST TENSE	=	FULL FORM	
wait	/weyt/	-ed	/əd/	waited	/weytəd/
wade	/weyd/	-ed	/əd/	waded	/weydəd/

This resumé accounts for past-tense forms of all verbs except some seventy "strong" verbs like bring, teach, choose, send, etc. These verbs do not obey the rules sketched above. (If they did, then we would have *bringed, teached, choosed, sended, i.e., /briŋd/,

/tiyčt/, /čuwzd/,/sendəd/. Some, like *do* and *be* follow rules that are strictly their own. Others, like *send* and *spend* or *drive* and *write* have rules for their own little groups.

The "he, she, it" forms of the verb in the present tense demonstrate analogous processes of affixation. When we say *he skips* /skips/ *he brags* /brægz/ and *he misses* /misəz/, we affix one or ther other of the present-tense allomorphs to the verb base. This present tense morpheme may be written {-z}, and its allomorphs are /s/,/z/, and /əz/.

These processes, then, exemplify the two basic kinds of morphemes, bases and affixes. It is true that some bases are not very productive. Similarly, some affixes are quite rare. But no matter. All English words are either simple (*hat, of, lavender*)—that is, they cannot be made any smaller—or they are complex (*hats, ran, blackboards*). All English words are made up of morphemes, either bases or affixes. We could represent this fact algebraically with a kind of formula:

$WORD$ = ±affix ± affix + *Base* ± affix ± affix ± affix

In other words, an English word can be a simple base (*hat, woman, lavender*), or it can be an affix + base (*return, dispose, hemisphere*), or it can be a base + affix (*hats, turning, lifelike*), and so on, up to *antidisestablishmentarianism,* which is about as packed with affixes as it is possible to be.

Intonational morphemes—forms that have some kind of meaning and that are built up of pitches, stresses, and junctures—are not overly complicated. They are attributes of English that go unnoticed, though, and are therefore rather mysterious at first sight. We have touched on this business before, so it won't be entirely arcane.

The pitch sequence /2/-/3/-/1/ (mid-to-high-to-low) that is associated with English "statements" is an intonational morpheme. The "some kind of meaning" that the sequence has is syntactic. Consider the following sentences:

He may want to see me later.

It's later than you think.

Two and two make four.

We speak these sentences with the characteristic /2/-/3/-/1/. Such a sequence of pitches means "statement." So the morpheme is written {2-3-1}. Now consider

He may want to see me later?

It's later than you think?

Two and two make four?

These "same" sentences are now different. They are now questions. The morpheme is {2-3}. Let's go on to

Do you think it'll rain?

Couldn't we talk about something else?

What do you think of them apples?

Where'd I put my hat?

The first two are "questions" with {2-3}. The last two are "questions" with {2-3-1}. Interesting!

Even more interesting are *stress morphemes*. Before we discover them together, let's say what we expect them to be technically. They will be sequences of stress that have some kind of meaning and that contrast with one another systematically. So, consider these phrases:

(1)	líght swìtch	(4)	lîght swítch	
(2)	cóok-oùt	(5)	cóok óut	
(3)	wríting-pàper	(6)	wrîting páper	

(1) is the switch that we use to turn lights on; (4) is a switch that doesn't weigh very much. (2) is hamburgers in the back yard; (5) is to plan for hamburgers in the back yard. (3) is stationery; (6) is paper that writes. Thus, the difference in meaning between (1) and (4) for example, is traceable to the difference in stresses; *ergo*, the difference is morphemic. {ˊ ˋ} is not {ˆ ˊ}.

Onward. To *morphophonemics.* That's a mouthful for what happens phonemically when morphemes brush up against one another. *How did you find me?* comes out something like

/hâwǰ ə f áynmiy/

in normal English. (One may believe that such a pronunciation is an abomination and belongs only in the mouths of those who would defile our noble tongue. But that opinion is of no importance here.) Speakers of English do not say sentences as if the words in them were in a list. They make automatic "accomodations" to neighboring sound as they go. *Here's your hat; what's your hurry?* is more like

/hîrẑərhǽt wôcerhə́riy/

than

/hír íz yúr hǽt hwát íz yúr hə́riy/

This sentence and the one preceding it illustrate a couple of the morphophonemic processes in English. In the case of *Here's you hat; what's your hurry?* the /z/ at the end of *Here's* followed immediately by the /y/ of *your* results in the blending of the two sounds into /ž/. In the same way, the /s/ at the end of *what's* followed directly by the /y/ at the beginning of *your* results in a morphophonemic change to /č/.

The morphophonemic processes involved in the affixation of the past-tense morpheme or the present-tense morpheme to verb bases have already been discussed (see pp. 36 to 38). We can look here at the *rules* for plural affixation. They are not unlike the rules for the third person present forms of the verb, that is, for the "he, she, it" forms. In general the rules for plural affixation are as follows: (1) singular nouns that end in voiceless consonants except /s/, /š/, and /č/ add /s/ to make the nouns plural; (2) singular nouns that end in voiced consonants except /z/, /ž/, and /ǰ/ add /z/ to make the nouns plural; (3) singular nouns that end in /s/, /z/, /š/, /ž/, /č/, and /ǰ/ add /əz/ to make the plural. Thus:

SINGULAR		+ PLURAL AFFIX	=	PLURAL
hat	/hæt/	/s/		/hæts/
pipe	/payp/	/s/		/payps/
chief	/čiyf/	/s/		/čiyfs/
lake	/leyk/	/s/		/leyks/

SINGULAR	+	PLURAL AFFIX	=	PLURAL
bib	/bib/	/z/		/bibz/
load	/lowd/	/z/		/lowdz/
key	/kiy/	/z/		/kiyz/
chair	/čer/	/z/		/čerz/
kiss	/kis/	/əz/		/kisəz/
badge	/bæǰ/	/əz/		/bæǰəz/

Morphophonemics not only covers what happens at morphemic boundaries; it also extends to internal change in words. Take *calf* and *half* for example. Each of these words has *two* allomorphs. The one that occurs before the plural morpheme is /kæv-/ or /hæv-/ respectively; the one that occurs everywhere else is /kæf-/ or /hæf-/. These facts can be represented in what is called "morphophonemic writing" as /kæF-/ or /hæF-/. The capital F means "either /f/ or /v/, depending." This same morphophoneme occurs not only in *calf* and *half*, but in *leaf* and *loaf*, *wife* and *knife*, and a few others. Similarly, words like *booth*, *bath*, *path*, and *wreath* exhibit a /θ/:/ð/ morphophonemic alternation that parallels the /f/:/v/ alternation in *calf*, *half*, etc.

Even with all of this, we still have only begun to scratch the surface of morphophonemics. The loss of the /t/ of *soft* in *soften*, the addition of /g/ to *long* in *longer*, the /s/:/z/ in *consist : resist*, and the alternation of *im-* and *in-* in *impossible* and *insecure* mark off some further morphophonemic processes. Beyond them lie the intriguing matters of *gradation*, where stress shifts accompany sound changes:

ócean	→	oceánic	cigár	→	cigarétte
maríne	→	máriner	córdial	→	cordiálity
áble	→	ability	anátomy	→	anatómical
régular	→	regulárity	mýstery	→	mystérious

Even this isn't the end. But let's pretend that it is.

Word classes are fun. The principle of analysis, as always, is observation and classification based on observable behavior. In English, the inflectional, derivational, and distributional behavior of words is taken as the classifying attribute. Forms that inflect, are derived, and are distributed in English sentences in identical ways are put together in a single *class*. (The presentation of word classes that follows is adapted from the work of Charles Carpenter Fries in his book *The Structure of English*, published by Harcourt, Brace, and World in 1952. Readers may wish to consult this book for a fuller account.)

Words like *concert, clerk, tax,* and *team* along with many others, form a class (1) because they inflect for the plural, and (2) because they distribute themselves in English sentences in identical ways. The virtue of a classification that is based on the recognition of such features of behavior is that it is foolproof. If we say that all forms that behave in such and such a way belong to a distinct class, then only those forms which behave in the prescribed way will be members of that class. The class of word headed by *concert, clerk, tax,* and *team* includes *man, fudgsicle, carnival, continent, elephant, market, marsupial,* and thousands of others. *They all inflect for the plural.*

(one)	concert	(two)	concerts
(one)	clerk	(two)	clerks
(one)	man	(two)	men
(one)	marsupial	(two)	marsupials

As to syntactic distribution, the members of this class will occur only in certain positions in English sentences, one of them being after *the: the fudgsicle, the man, the tax,* etc. They will also occur in the positions exemplified below:

my concerts	great carnivals	Sue's market
my taxes	great continents	Sue's clerk
my elephant	great teams	Sue's syntax

The whole class we call *Class 1.*

A second class of word in English is that class of forms which (1) inflect for the third-person-present tense, (2) inflect for the past tense, and (3) distribute themselves in their own little niches in English sentences. Such words as *remember, go, decide, spell, announce* and a good many others meet the test of these three rules.

he remembers	he remembered	let's remember
he goes	he went	let's go
he decides	he decided	let's decide

Words that follow these patterns of structure belong to *Class 2.* Notice what happens when these two classes are turned upside down.

```
*my remembers          *let's carnival
*my goes               *let's continent
*my decides            *let's team
```

None of these works out. Of course, it is possible to be an English word and belong to more than one class.

```
the clerk              he clerked
the tax                he taxed (them)
my face                I faced (them)
```

The words after *the* in the left-hand column belong to *Class 1;* the words after the pronouns in the right-hand column belong to *Class 2.*

Words like *old, rough, pretty, sullen,* and *huge* are members of a third class of word. Not only these but also *older, prettier,* and *roughest* belong to the same class. Just as both *concert* and *concerts* belong to *class 1; old, older,* and *oldest* belong to this *Class 3* group. These words (1) inflect for the "comparative" and the "superlative" (*-er* and *-est*), and (2) occupy only certain positions in English sentences.

All the italicized words in the sentence below and any form that will substitute for any of them without changing the structural meaning of the sentence belong to *Class 4.*

> *Perhaps* they have *never yet* run *back*
> *upstairs quickly enough, however.*

They all share either features of inflection or position that no other class has.

These four large classes are "open-ended"; that is, they freely add words to their groups. Each day brings new members. Then too, some others are lost.

(The reader has not been fooled in the least by any of this. "Oh, he's just talking about nouns, verbs, adjectives, and adverbs." Of course. These words are as good as any to refer to the classes. But nothing has been said about words that are "names of persons, places, and things," or words that "express action," or words that "modify the meanings" of other words. If we play that game, then we can make *up* a noun because it is the name of a direction, or we can make *tornado* a verb because it is a word that expresses action, or we can make *let's* an adverb in *Let's dance* because it is a word that modifies a verb. This game we will leave to prescientific grammars. Instead, we will content ourselves with an insistence on dealing with observable behavioral features of forms in our classification procedures.)

There remain several other groups of words to be classified. These are "closed groups" that admit no new members.

The first such group is that headed by *the* and *a*. This group, which includes *any, every, my, no, one, two, some* and *Mr. Smith's*, is established on the basis of the *same* criterion of distributional characteristics that was used, in part, to establish the four *form classes* above. The question here is "Which words pattern the way *the* and *a* do." In part, the answer will be made evident in the listing below.

the	boy	*any*	street	*Mr. Smith's*	houses
a	boy	*this*	street	*two*	houses
my	boy	*every*	street	*no*	houses
his	boy	*our*	street	*some*	houses
her	boy	*your*	street	*their*	houses

This is not the end of the list, but it is nearly so. What we are dealing with are two-word phrases that have *Class 1* words in the second position. The words that fill the left-hand position are the members of the present group, call it *Group A*. *Pretty* and *ugly* do not belong to this group because even though each will occur where *the* and *a* do, they share, as we saw a moment or two ago, certain inflectional characterictics (*pretty, prettier, prettiest*) that none of the present group does.

Group B is headed by *is* and *was*. Each occurs before a *Class 2* word. Some examples are

can do	*is* studying
could help	*must* concertize
got going	*will* ratify
has gone	*was* congealed

Group C contains one morpheme, in either its free form /nat/ or its bound forms /ənt/or/nt/, namely {*not*}.

Group D is headed by *very*. The members of the group occur only before *Class 3* words. They are often called "intensifiers".

very uncommon	*more* often	*quite* right
awfully good	*most* casual	*rather* quiet
even more	*pretty* ugly	*some* better

There are others, but not too many. (Notice that *too* in the preceding sentence is a member of *Group D*.)

Group E has *and, but, nor* and *or,* as well as *both . . . and, either . . . or, neither . . . nor, neither . . . or,* and *not . . . but.*

Group F has *at, by, concerning, during, from, to, with,* and all other words that pattern like them in English phrases. Some of their distributional features are suggested in the following listing:

at night	*until* tomorrow	*through* the middle
by day	*from* here	*with* much gusto
in school	*to* there	*beyond* his competence

Group G has just *do, does,* and *did.*

Do you do your work?	*Do* you dance?
Does he do his work?	*Does* she, or *does*n't she?
Did he do his work?	*Did* he take the test?

Group H, like *Group C,* has just one member, *there.* It is usually weakly stressed, and it only distributes itself with forms of the verb *to be.*

There's an interesting person here.
There is some mustard on my shirt.
There will be a short recess now.

Group I forms its membership with *who, which, when, what, how, that, why,* and *where,* along with their derivatives.

Why do the prudent fall?
Where did he go?
Why are you here?
How are you?

Group J has all words that function in the place occupied by *because* in *He helped because I couldn't,*

because
but
although
He helped *when* I couldn't.
so
since

This group includes those words that mark what are called "included sentences":

A story *that* I know.
A place *which* is quiet.
Women *whom* we adore.

Group K has a small membership, just *now, oh, well,* and *why.*

> *Now* stop that.
> *Oh* I don't know.
> *Well* that's that.

These words are nearly equivalent to the *hems* and *haws* that are sprinkled through everyone's speech.

Group L has *yes* and *no. Group M* has *please.* And *Group N* has *let's.* That's the end.

These fourteen *function groups* are extremely important in English syntax. We could hardly do without them. Main ideas and principal syntax come from the arrangements of *Class 1-4* words. But the delicate balancing and directing of phrase against phrase and the clarifying of syntactic construction come from the maneuvering of *Group A-N* words.

No word belongs to any form class or function group before somebody says something. Syntactic function is a function of use, in this sense. Words in sentences have functions, not words on lists or words hanging in mid-space. Look at the following:

> 1
> It's third *down* and four to go.

> 4
> Put it *down.*

> F
> They live *down* the street.

> 2
> Their halfback *downed* the ball.

Here's one word that is used in four different syntactic ways, as a *Class 1* word, as a *Class 4* word, as a *Group F* word, and as a *Class 2* word.

The analysis of English words into eighteen "parts of speech" permits the analysis of any sentence, theoretically. Two minutes ago I asked my wife to let me see the book she was reading. She gave it to me, and my eyes fell first on the following sentence (the analysis is provided):

> A 3   1   4   1   2 4 F A   2
> A little while later, Faye drove by in her battered

> 1   2   1 E   2   F A   1   A
> Ford touring car and pulled into the curb some

>   A   1   4
> twenty feet away.

It would also be possible to conduct a phonemic, a morphological, and a morphemic analysis of this same sentence. If we did, we would have begun to unravel the mystery of what it is made of. Coupled with the part-of-speech analysis, we would have laid bare a good deal of the physical structure of the sentence, and we would be well on our way to a more or less complete description of the structure of the thing. But there is still more to do.

With part-of-speech analysis behind us, we can attend to *syntax* itself. This study deals with the relationships that words enter into in sentences. As before, the technique of analysis emphasizes recognition of recurring patterns of structure. In this case, the structural linguist looks for patterns of arrangement involving the distribution of the members of the form classes and function groups. Imagine that the linguist has collected phrases like those below from his English informant.

1 a pigeon
2 the ranks
3 every funeral
4 his friends

It is possible, isn't it, to generalize upon such structures, to say that (1) they consist of two forms, syntactically, (2) the first form is a member of *Group A* (3) the second is a member of *Class 1*, and (4) the two forms occur in the order *Group A + Class 1*. Recalling the technical terminology from pages 27 to 28, we can say that each is a *noun phrase,* that the *Class 1* word is the *head* of the construction. and that the *Group A* word is the *satellite.* We can also say that each phrase has two constituents, each in the immediate environment of the other. They are *immediate constituents.*

Now look at these phrases:

5 the entire program
6 a foolish politician
7 the open sky
8 all three languages

These phrases share some of the features of the first four. But there are observable differences. Considering that we have called the first four noun phrases, we cannot call phrases 5 through 8 noun phrases unless we broaden the "definition." This is easy enough, and it is useful. Otherwise, we would have more technical terminology than is really necessary. At bottom, the second four phrases are sufficiently like the first four to be called noun phrases. All eight phrases share the significant and essential syntactic features of *Class 1* as head plus one or more function groups as satellites.

Most immediate constituents are "binary," that is, there are two of them. If we have a two-word phrase, then the immediate constituents *(ICs)* are obvious:

If there are three words in the phrase, the ICs will still be binary though:

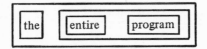

(These Chinese boxes are often used to display the ICs.) In more complicated phrases, the trick is to keep track of the deep structures. In a sentence like *The local newspaper is a stupid rag,* the basic syntactic elements are *The newspaper / is a rag.* The highest-level ICs in the sentence are the subject and the predicate:

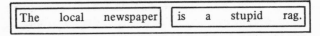

In this way, the ICs of the sentence are marked off all the way down to the word level; that is, the "relationships that words enter into" are analyzed and displayed. *Modification* becomes a "strategy" of head words and satellites; *conjunction* becomes a "coordination" of *Class* words and *Group E* words; *predication* becomes the "alignment" of noun phrases and verb phrases with special "link-ups" between them.

MODIFICATION

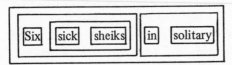

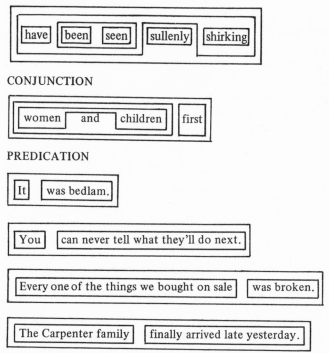

CONJUNCTION

PREDICATION

These last constructions are the same on the highest level of construction: subject + predicate. Not all high-level constructions are of this sort, however. Many English sentences are nonpredications, like *Oh, dear me, no:* or *Tony's wife* or *Which is what we are all talking about.* "Sentence," then, is a tricky thing. Put it this way. There are a very large number of high-level constructions in the English language that share one important structural feature: they are all marked off at the end by a terminal juncture. By virtue of this simple behavioral feature, they all belong to a single class of constructions. We can call the class *sentence.* In this way, *sentence* is like the chemist's *compound.* If the chemist is dealing with a substance that has more than one chemical element, he is dealing with a compound. If the linguist is dealing with structures that have terminal junctures, he says he is dealing with sentences.

Having arrived at the sentence, the outer bound of structural analysis, we come to the end of this sketch of the structure of

English. The structural features of English and the methodology for uncovering them are the subject that have found their way into English classrooms. In chemistry classrooms children familiarize themselves with the techniques that chemists use to penetrate the mysteries of our chemical world. They also learn something of the results of the practice of chemistry. In our social studies programs students are introduced to the tools of history and sociology. They are also led to learn some of the results of the use of these tools. So it is with English—and more, as we will see in the following chapter. It is possible to design a technique for the analysis of a language. It is also possible to persuade students who have learned such a technique to put it to use in their own investigations of language. In doing these two things, students equip themselves with an indispensable knowledge and a means to acquire more knowledge. Knowledge, they say, is good. The New English espouses these goals and ideals.

A long time ago, Thomas Hobbes said:

> Words are wise men's counters,—
> they do but reckon by them; but they
> are the money of fools.

Indeed, we "reckon" with words. And as Hobbes says, it is a shame that some would make a "foolish currency" of them.

We should know them and make them a "wise currency."

4 | GRAMMAR IN A NEW KEY

The question arises, "Why should grammar be taught?" Answers have ranged from "It's good for the soul" to "It makes better citizens of our youth." The likelihood of the first being substantiated is more than a little remote; the chances of the second being true are not good. It is not impossible that a connection exists between competence in grammar and enlightened citizenship even though no such relationship has ever been demonstrated. Still, answers such as these in effect beg the question. It is best to look for justification in teaching grammar in the clearer light of a more fundamental idea of teaching. An informed understanding of one's humanity is a common defense for teaching this or that other subject to children. Presumably history, literature, language, science art, and mathematics are taught youth because students are thereby in more direct command of their own lives. So much of our *humanity* is ours through language that it is hardly conceivable that education could do without language. A grammar that does a good job explaining language would therefore seem to require no further justification as a school subject. Even so, the subject is worth pursuing of and for itself. Learning chemistry is worthwhile just for the sake of learning chemistry quite apart from whether such knowledge has any practical value. In a sense, it's rather like the mountain climber who attempts to explain why he climbed the mountain by saying "It was there." Why should any student want to learn about math or history or language? Well, one reason is that they are there. By definition, the educated person is the one who has a decent respect for learning and knowledge. In this light, knowledge of language is a reasonable expectation for a school program to have.

The next question is "What grammar should be taught?" The question presupposes a choice of grammars. And so there is. Until fairly recently, there was only one grammar, so-called traditional grammar. In actuality, however, it was *not* traditional, scholarly grammar that was taught in the schools. What was taught might better have been called "school grammar." It was not the finely tuned grammar that had been produced over a fairly long period of time and was consummated in a number of full traditional grammars of English, among them Otto Jespersen's seven-volume *A Modern English Grammar on Historical Principles*, George Curme's *A Grammar of the English Language*, Hendrik Poutsma's *A Grammar of Late Modern English*, and Etsko Kruisinga's *A Handbook of Present-Day English*. No school, so far as I know, has undertaken to teach these full traditional-historical grammars of English. Instead, numberless adaptations of them found their way into textbook form for school use. Adaptation is really not the right word; bastardization would be fairer, if severer. For the most part, they were faulty representations of careful traditional-historical technique presented frequently with gross oversimplifications and such thinness as to be useless. Even the good in them was usually obscured by irrelevant and trivial sections on good manners on the telephone and decorum in the library, hopelessly esoteric and maudlin guides to literature, and, of course, pretty pictures. Grammar itself became lost in a variety of other topics, frequently becoming no more than one of several exercises following a reading or a composition assignment, showing up again toward the end in a review section where the old chestnuts about *Do's* and *Don't's* could be encountered for the umpteenth time. Today, no one with any sense seriously proposes to teach *this* grammar.

But again, "What grammar?" Considering the answer to the first question, that an understanding of language is one of the foundations of knowledge, the answer to this question must be "That grammar that has the best chance of explaining language." This is a very delicate matter, for two reasons. First, it has not been made clear even among English linguists which of several grammars is the most powerful in this regard; and second, even if one particular grammar could be irrefutably established as the most powerful one, it would not follow necessarily that it should or could be taught children and adolescents.

Let me explain. First there is this matter of alternative grammars. Not everyone will be ready to believe that there is more than one grammar of English. But remember that the structural model presented in Chapter Three is a *grammar*. And then there is the traditional grammar. That makes two. In fact, it is axiomatic that there are optional theories of grammar and optional grammars. That is, it is possible to ask, "What *form* shall a grammar take?" This question always follows the observation that in some sense speakers of a language have *internalized* a "grammar" of their native language. I have touched on this matter indirectly before (Chapter Two), but it needs to be explained here that the term "grammar" has at least two meanings: (1) grammar is the knowledge that a speaker has that enables him to say and write intelligible things and to interpret what he hears and reads; (2) grammar is a formal study of this speaker-knowledge that results in a set of statements of whatever length that "reports" the knowledge. Now, considering this second sense of grammar, the question is, "Are there alternative sets of statements that report the knowledge that a speaker has?" The answer is an emphatic *Yes!* The most familiar grammar is the one mentioned above—the school grammar. It is this one that cautioned us to mind our *P's* and *Q's*. Traditional grammar gave us the names of English grammatical categories—*sentence, noun, past participle,* and so forth. Structural grammar, the one discussed in the preceding chapter, takes overt linguistic data and analyzes it objectively. There is yet another grammar; that is, there is yet another answer to the question of what form a grammar shall take. This grammar is called *transformational-generative grammar.* It seeks to explicitly characterize the sentences that people say in terms of the knowledge they have about them. And it is this grammar that I wish to describe now, so that later on we can see how it is being taught and how it and structural grammar are also being used to teach "non-grammatical" elements in The New English.

Transformation-Generative Grammar

Suppose for the moment that the English language had only the following grammatical sentences:

1. The boy chases the girl.
2. The girl chases the boy.
3. A boy chases a girl.
4. A girl chases a boy.
5. A boy chases the girl.
6. A girl chases the boy.
7. A boy chases a boy.
8. The boy chases the boy.
9. A girl chases a girl.
10. The girl chases the girl.
11. A boy chases the boy.
12. A girl chases the girl.
13. The girl cries.
14. A girl cries.
15. The boy cries.
16. A boy cries.
17. The girl laughs.
18. A girl laughs.
19. The boy laughs.
20. A boy laughs.

And suppose that it had none of the following non-grammatical sentences:

21. *The boy chases.
22. *A boy chases.
23. *The girl chases.
24. *A girl chases.
25. *The boy laughs the girl.
26. *The girl laughs the boy.
27. *A boy laughs a girl.
28. *A girl laughs a boy.
29. *The boy cries the boy.
30. *The girl cries the girl.
etc.

Now here's the problem. Write a grammar that will specify sentences 1 through 20 as grammatical and sentences 21 through 30 as non-grammatical. Write a grammar that will *enumerate* just sentences 1 through 20. Write a set of statements of some kind that will *generate* none of sentences 21 through 30 but all of sentences 1 through 20. Write a grammar that will explicitly characterize all the sentences of a language and none of the non-sentences. That's four ways of putting the same thing. The transformational-generative approach writes a grammar that is requested in the four directions above.

Let's make a beginning of a characterization of such a grammar. If we could write a "rule" that would prevent *chases* from occurring in any sentence that lacks an object, and if we could write a rule that would meanwhile prevent *laughs* and *cries* from occurring in any sentence that has an object, we would be on the right track, because these constraints would mean first that we wouldn't generate any sentence of the kind **The boy chases*, nor, in the second case, any sentence of the kind **The boy laughs the girl*. The other thing that would have to be done is the automatic selection of both *the* and *a*—only one at a time, though—before both *boy* and *girl*. (Traditional grammar has no way of doing these things. Neither does structural grammar. Either can handily describe the structure of any of sentences 1 through 20, but again, neither would utter a syllable about non-sentences 21 through 30. The grammar that sets as its goals (1) the automatic specification of the sentences of a language and (2) the automatic rejection of the non-grammatical sentences is transformational-generative grammar. One of the reasons it is designed this way is that it imposes as a minimum requirement the enumeration of all of the sentences but also none of the non-sentences. It sets this low-level goal for itself because, by achieving it, it would succeed in accounting for a competence that the speakers of the language have. *Speakers know which sentences are well-formed and which aren't!* At the same time, such a grammar as this, if it succeeded, would explicitly explain how it is that an infinite number of sentences are the product of the finite means of a language.

Now, back to the problem at hand. What does a grammar look like that will "generate" sentences 1 through 20 while it fails, deliberately and explicitly, to "generate" sentences 21 through 30. We noted above that a grammar that would permit certain constructions but deny others would be on the right track. We can observe now that one way to do this would be to establish an ordered set of "rules." Suppose we said that all well-formed sentences in the language under view (the language with just sentences 1 through 20) consist of a *noun phrase* followed by a *verb phrase*. This would be an accurate statement because each of sentences 1 through 20 contains a noun phrase and a verb phrase in that order. Sentence (2), for example, *The boy chases the girl*, contains the noun phrase *The boy* and the verb phrase *chases the girl*. A rule that would say that *all* sentences have this structure might look like this:

$$S \rightarrow NP + VP$$

This formulation is an instruction to rewrite S(entence) as N(oun) P(hrase) + V(erb) P(hrase). This is Rule 1.

$$1.\ S \rightarrow NP + VP$$

Rule 2 can be formulated as follows:

$$2.\ NP \rightarrow A + N$$

This rule says rewrite N(oun) P(hrase) as A(rticle) + N(oun). The rule will give us such phrases as *The boy, a girl*, etc., in which *the* and *a* are the articles and *boy* and *girl* are the nouns.

Let's stop at this point and see where we are and where we are headed. If we examine Rule 1, we note that sentences 1 through 20 will be enumerated if we can straighten out what goes where in the noun phrases (*The boy, a girl*, etc.,) and the verb phrases (*chases a boy, cries*, etc.). Then, an examination of Rule 2 will indicate that all of the noun phrases that we are talking about in Rule 1 will be of the kind A + N (*a boy, the girl*, and so forth). We are zeroing in on the structures of the sentences. Everything will be all right if we can successfully sort out the problem of the verbs: *chases* never ends a sentence, but *cries* and *laughs* always do.

Here's Rule 3.

$$3.\ VP \rightarrow \begin{Bmatrix} Vt + NP \\ Vi \end{Bmatrix}$$

This complex formulation says: Rewrite the V(erb) P(hrase) as *either* V(erb) t(ransitive) + N(oun) P(hrase) *or* as V(erb) i(nstransitive). When items are written in brackets, the instruction is to select *one or the other,* never both. *Transitive* verbs are the ones that "take objects." *Intransitive* verbs are the ones that do not.

Things are getting interesting, aren't they? Notice what has happened. We have now required that the V(erb) P(hrase) from Rule 1 can only appear as Vt + NP (*chases the girl, chases a boy*, and so forth) *or* as Vi (*laughs, cries*)—or at least we have begun to say these things. We must now specify *chases* as V(erb) t(ransitive) and *laughs* and *cries* as V(erb) i(ntransitive).

4. Vt → *Chases*
5. Vi → *cries, laughs*

So much for that little problem. Now let's clear up the nouns and the articles.

6. A → *the, a*
7. N → *boy, girl*

So much for most of the problems. We have succeeded in writing rules that will generate all and only the well-formed sentences that we started with. Here are the rules all together.

1. S → NP + VP

2. NP → A + N

3. VP → $\begin{Bmatrix} Vt + NP \\ Vi \end{Bmatrix}$

4. Vt → *chases*

5. Vi → *cries, laughs*

6. A → *the, a*

7. N → *boy, girl*

These rules will enumerate all of sentences 1 through 20 and none of sentences 21 through 30.

Let's follow the generation of one or two sentences. In order to interpret Rule 2 (NP → A + N), we must consult Rules 6 and 7. These rules have choices, exactly the condition we want considering the sentences we are after. If we select *the* for A and *boy* for N, then we will have *the boy* for NP. But which NP? The one in Rule 1 or the one in Rule 3? It doesn't matter. If we select the Vi of Rule 3, the question won't even come up because then we'll necessarily have a sentence with only one NP, namely, *the subject.* But if we select

Vt + NP in Rule 3, then the sentence will automatically have two NPs because we will be dealing with a sentence of the kind NP + Vt + NP. This will mean that we will have to follow Rules 6 and 7 twice. If we select *the* for A and *girl* for N this time, we will have projected the sentence *The boy chases the girl*, and that's one of the sentences we want.

Or again, this time from the beginning. Rule 1 specifies that whatever sentence we end up with, it will have a NP followed by a VP, that is, a noun phrase followed by a verb phrase. Rule 2 requires that each NP take the form A + N, that is, article followed by noun. Now, for Rule 3 let's select the option Vi. In other words, the VP must appear now as an intransitive verb. We therefore bypass Rule 4 because there is no Vt in the derivation. For Rule 5, let's select *cries*. For Rule 6, let's select *a* and for Rule 7, let's choose *boy*. Following the rules in this particular way results in the grammatical sentence *A boy cries*.

Are you perplexed dear reader? Are you a grown man crying because you are lost? Fret not. Return to the listing of the rules in order on page 57 and see whether you can determine that, in fact, these rules when scrupulously followed will generate sentences 1 through 20 but not sentences 21 through 30.

One thing, I hope, is fairly clear. A grammar of this kind, however mysterious it seems upon first encounter, is a grammar that formally specifies the well-formed sentences of a language by constructing rules of the kind sketched above. If you are of a mind to worry over it a bit longer, an effort to follow the development of such rules as presented on pages 55 to 57 will be rewarding.

It is a relatively simple matter to design such a grammar for a language that has only twenty sentences, especially when the twenty sentences are so much alike. It is another matter to produce such a grammar for a natural language like English. Even so, a generative grammar is theoretically possible. We could increase the power of the grammar for those twenty sentences by merely increasing the vocabulary. By adding *this* and *that* to Rule 6, and by adding *man, woman, fox, wolf, American, Canadian,* and even *flying saucer* to the options in Rule 7, we can empower the grammar to generate tens of thousands of sentences, all of them perfectly well-formed:

This flying saucer chases that Canadian.
That flying saucer chases this flying saucer.
This fox chases this wolf.
That wolf chases a woman.
The woman chases the man.
And so on.

We would still be talking about a grammar with *seven rules*! Such a grammar is worth serious consideration.

So far though, we have only sketched the surface of one part of transformational-generative grammar. In fact, we have been looking at the generative part only. What about the transformational part?

We'll begin as we did before, with a few English sentences:

31. The boy chased the girl.
32. The girl chased the boy.
33. The girl was chased by the boy.
34. The boy was chased by the girl.

If we look closely, we see that sentence 31 is a version of sentence 33 and that sentence 32 is a version of sentence 34. Furthermore, the pairs are versions of one another *in the same ways*. An old-fashioned way of putting it is that sentences 31 and 33 "say the same thing." So do sentences 32 and 34. A more technical way of phrasing it is to say that the *active* sentences (31 and 32) *are related formally* to the *passive* sentences (33 and 34). The English language exhibits this formal property systematically. Sentences 1 through 12 are all active sentences that have passive, mirror-image sentences just like sentences 33 and 34. Indeed, most active sentences like *The boy chased the girl* have their passive mates in *The girl was chased by the boy*.

35. Pamela empties all the ashtrays.
36. All the ashtrays are emptied by Pamela.
37. I tolerated his insolence.
38. His insolence was tolerated by me.
39. The football broke the window.
40. The window was broken by the football.

But notice:

41. The boy hid the box.
42. The box was hidden by the boy.
43. The baby weighed ten pounds.
44. *Ten pounds was weighed by the baby.

Only one of the readings of sentence 42 applies to sentence 41, that the boy hid the box. The other reading, that it was the boy who obscured our vision of the box, suggests that the relationship between sentences 41 and 42 is not the same as the relationship between sentences 43 and 44, or between sentences 35 and 36, 37 and 38, and 39 and 40. Superficially, there is the same parallelism, but deep down somewhere there is an important difference in these pairs. (We'll return to the *surface structure vs. deep structure* a little later.)

Considering all sentences in English like

> 31. The boy chased the girl.
> 33. The girl was chased by the boy.

(1) The grammar must specify that the sentences are related, and (2) it must indicate what the relationship is. Here is where the *transformation* part comes in. We must write a rule that will automatically transform sentence 31 into sentence 33, or for that matter, all sentences like 31 into all sentences like 33. For the purposes of this discussion, let's write the rule this way:

$$T1. \quad NP_1 + Vt + NP_2 \quad \Rightarrow \quad NP_2 + AUX + Vt + by + NP_1$$

T1 means *transformation rule 1.*
NP_1 and NP_2 mean *the first and second* NP's *in the active sentence, respectively.*
$\Rightarrow$ means *becomes by structural change.*
AUX means *auxilliary verb.*
by is the English word *by.*

A display of how this transformational rule works may be helpful:

$$NP_1 \quad + \quad Vt \quad + \quad NP_2 \Rightarrow$$
The boy   chased   the girl.

$$NP_2 \quad + \quad AUX \quad + \quad Vt \quad + \quad by \quad + \quad NP_1$$
The girl   was   chased   by   the boy.

Another example of transformation will make the process clearer. Suppose we had begun all this with

> 1. $S \rightarrow NP + VP \ (ADV)$

where (ADV) meant "optional adverb". Now if we had had sentences like

The boy chased the girl.
The boy chased the girl yesterday.
The girl chased the boy.
The girl chased the boy yesterday.

and so forth, we would have needed the rule

8. ADV → *yesterday*

which would have guaranteed the generation of all such sentences.

Now, if we had also had sentences like

The boy chased the girl.
Yesterday, the boy chased the girl.
The girl chased the boy.
Yesterday, the girl chased the boy.

and so forth, how could we get the grammar to account for these sentences? The answer is that we would do this by introducing the following transformational rule:

T2. NP + VP (ADV) ⇒ (ADV) NP + VP

We read this transformational rule as: N(oun) P(hrase) + V(erb) P(hrase) + optional ADV(erb) *becomes by structural change* optional ADV(erb) + N(oun) P(hrase) + V(erb) P(hrase).

Thus, by ordering what are called *phrase structure rules* and *transformational rules*, each of the kind X→Y+Z, a transformational-generative grammar characterizes all the sentences in a language—syntactically. But notice that the sounds and the meanings have been left uncharacterized. When we remember that a language is a pairing of sound and sense, we see that only one job has been done with the specification of the syntax.

As to the sound system in a language, *phonology*, recent work indicates very strongly that phonetic representations will be in terms of universal phonetic symbols. Each sound will be described as having or as not having one of the two members of a distinct pairing of phonetic features. The sound [p] in English will be described as having *voicelessness* and as not having *voice*; it will be described as being *consonantal* but as not being *vocalic*. [b], shown below with [p], is also marked according to this scheme.

	[p]	[b]
voiceless	+	−
voice	−	+
consonantal	+	+
vocalic	−	−

On an elevated level of analysis, one of the things that a phonological component might do for English is specify the permissible combination of sounds that form English words, while rejecting the non-permissible combinations. Doing this would again reflect the competence that speakers of English have. The list below will provide the data that will permit us to examine this possibility.

1. tall
2. ball
3. mall
4. pall
5. crawl
6. stall
7. fall
8. *nall
9. *sall
10. *ndall

In this list words 1 through 7 are all "permissible" phonetic combinations; words 8 through 10 are not "permissible." Speakers of English would know that 8 and 9 *could* be English words but that 10 could not possibly be. It is *anomalous*, phonetically. An adequate grammar would carefully distinguish these groups.

The really important work of the phonological component of a transformational-generative grammar would be to provide phonetic information for the sentences that the syntactic component generates. It would provide phonetic *readings*.

The phonetic description and the syntactic description of a sentence provide what is called the "input" to the semantic component (meaning) which in turn places a semantic interpretation upon the sentence. It works something like this:

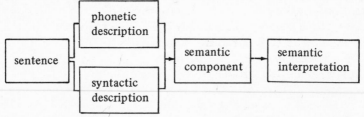

A brief description of the semantic component of a transformational-generative grammar is now in order. A short sentence like

45. People lined the street.

will serve as a jumping-off place. The syntactic description of the sentence, using what is called a "branching tree diagram", will show

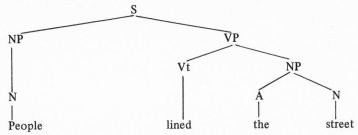

The phonetic description will specify the sounds, the pitches, the junctures, etc. But neither the syntactic description nor the phonetic description will say anything about what the sentence *means* (in the usual sense of the term). The semantic component will "read" the input from the syntactic and the phonetic descriptions and will provide an interpretation of the meaning. The problem with sentence 45 is that it is semantically ambiguous. It has more than one meaning. According to one reading, *some people have marked lines on the street,* and according to another, *the people have placed themselves in lines along the sides of the street.* In other words,

46. People lined the streets with yellow paint.

is related to one of the readings of sentence 45, while

47. People lined the street six deep.

is related to the other reading. But we are left with what to do with sentence 45. Any adequate grammar of English must be able to detect its ambiguity and must supply the appropriate readings. Similarly, such a grammar must have the capacity to detect anomalous sentences like

48. *People lined the street with their vacations.
49. *Two and two are taller than I am.
50. *The horse was a mammal.

The following observations should be no surprise: the semantic component reflects the ability the speakers have; they know when sentences are ambiguous or anomalous. It is the job of the part of the grammar that assigns meanings to sentences to know the same. Two sub-components of the semantic component energize this capacity: a special dictionary and a set of special rules. The dictionary entry for *line* would be quite different from the familiar entries in desk dictionaries, and it would automatically force a double reading of sentence 45. The entry for *line*, Vt, would look like this:

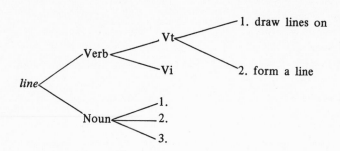

So, when *People lined the street* gets to this subcomponent, it would automatically be interpreted in two ways. Suffice it to say of the other sub-component, the *special rules*, that the rules would be ordered sets of directions. All the paths and tracings through the dictionary would be clearly marked.

We can grasp something of the gigantic complexity of this component by considering a deceptively simple little sentence like

> 51. That line is mine.

There are probably hundreds of readings for this sentence, ranging from

	51a.	That mark on the paper is mine.
and	51b.	That extension phone is mine.
to	51c.	That line of sports equipment is mine.
and	51d.	That group of people in front of my desk is mine.

but not 51e. *That date line is mine.

It is no simple task to produce the kind of grammar that we are presently considering. It is a fairly easy task, however, to describe the requirements of the grammar. It should (1) reflect what people know about their language, (2) enumerate all the sentences of the language, and (3) specify the syntactic, phonological, and semantic make-up of all the sentences. No small task, but one very much worth pursuing, if only because it sets its goals so high.

Structural Grammar in the Classroom

The first point that must be made is that all of the facts about English that were presented in Chapter Three are learned by children. In gradually more difficult and more comprehensive lessons over a period of many years, the youth are guided through a formal inquiry into the phonological, morphological, and syntactic systems of English. They learn to talk about how their language works. (To *know* their language.) All of the instruction and the learning is structure-centered: it is about the language *per se*. Beyond it lie the rich harvests of numerous applications, the most compelling being the acquisition of an informed attitude on linguistic matters. Knowing a good deal about how language works (in particular their own), understanding much about the scientific approach to study and investigation, and appreciating the power that comes from knowledge and the satisfaction that flows from useful work, students come to look upon their experience in school as one that sets them free to learn for themselves. That school that merely imparts information or that only maintains discipline is no school at all. Schools are places where the heat rises in direct proportion to the number of engaged brains.

Beyond this first-order application of modern grammar are very many specific lessons and exercises, some examples of which we can get to in a moment. But here we can sketch an overview of general application.

First, there is composition. The structural analysis of English has resulted in the description of certain recurrent and basic sentence patterns. In brief, it has been shown that practically all predications in English (the familiar subject + predicate constructions) reduce to a mere half-dozen or so fundamental arrangements. Recognition of this fact has led to a number of exercises that encourage students to identify these basic patterns of arrangement and to produce them deliberately in writing.

Second, reading can be taught with an eye to pattern and form. Authors cast their ideas in the same sentence patterns mentioned above (this sentence, for example, which has *authors* as subject and all the rest as predicate). Thus, techniques have been introduced in the teaching of reading that encourage students to identify syntactic groups as they read. Such techniques have been shown to increase both speed and comprehension in reading.

Third, the structural analysis of great numbers of natural languages has led many to suppose that structural techniques can be used in the teaching of foreign languages. One thing has been made clear, at least until such time as universal grammar is codified, and that is that there is no such thing as "English grammar for foreign students." An English grammar for Spanish speakers will be very different from an English grammar for Japanese speakers. But here the important point is that there are millions of youngsters in this country who in effect are learning standard English in school as if it were a foreign language. The "culturally disadvantaged" youth are in English or "language arts" classrooms as second-language speakers of standard English. Despite the fact that some school districts are not only backward but perniciously stupid about how to teach "disadvantaged" children (as reported, for example, by Jonathan Kozol in his *Death at an Early Age*), modern structuralism has invigorated "remedial"programs all across the country. The reader with a special interest in this problem may wish to consult *Nonstandard Speech and the Teaching of English* (published by the Center for Applied Linguistics in 1964).

The position that structuralism has taken on usage has lifted the pall of authoritarian instruction and has actually reversed what was a deplorable course. The culturally different child is no longer accused of being a willful linguistic delinquent or of being "wrong" every time he opens his mouth to say "Him and me, we don't got none." With an enlightened point of view, his teacher can now (1) appreciate that there is just as much grammar in his sentence as there is in "We don't have any"—it's just different grammar, (2) approach the student's "problem" positively by encouraging him to look upon his own styles of language as an enormous achievement, and (3) persuade him to learn a different dialect from the one that he has grown up speaking and in which he rightly takes so much pride, not supposing that "We don't got none" is better linguistically than "We don't have any" or vice versa since it is perfectly obvious that good, bad, and indifferent are decided on social grounds, not linguistic ones. He doesn't have to be told that he'll get a crack on the head if he goes around saying "We don't have any" at home. (Smart-aleck college kids who have served in the army know all about this double standard. Sergeants are not amused by "standard" usage.) For practical, social purposes (among others), students can decide on their own that it's a good idea to know lots of dialects and styles of speech. No door to any dialect should be shut in the face of any student. To put it more colorfully: no dialect shouldn't never be shut to no student no time! Standard English serves a young American very well. Let him find it. Nonstandard English in its myriad forms also serves us very well. If we don't know them, then we know much less than we could!

The climate for instruction today is one of door-opening. Open the door to the language of poets, of politicians, of advertisers, of sports broadcasters, of teachers, of children, OF EVERYBODY—and the disadvantaged child, any child, will step inside to listen. Equip him with the means to conduct a useful analysis of these different styles, and he will learn something about himself and his fellow Americans.

Fourth, there is the trivial matter of spelling. The impact that modern modes of analysis have had on teaching spelling has been to relate comprehensively the correspondence between English sounds and English spelling. There is a more or less regular correspondence between the sounds of English and typical spelling. Ninety-nine of one hundred English words that have an f sound in them ($/f/$), are spelled with an f or two f's *(fit, after, cuff, etc.)*. The one in a hundred that isn't has a *ph (Philadelphia)* or a *gh (enough, rough)*. The teaching of English spelling becomes a matter, then, of first blocking out some forty or fifty regular patterns of correspondence between the sound system and the writing system, and then of treating the irregular relationships as minor patterns of correspondence. One of the significant results of this plan has been to revamp spelling lists. No longer is a child just dumped into the middle of what seems to him a hopelessly idiotic non-system of English spelling where on the same day he must learn to spell:

was	book	paper
of	could	fence
poem	dust	duty
spoon	animal	garage

Now, as I say, the regular material is learned first:

hat	sat	fat
mat	cat	rat

bite	side	wide
kite	file	mine
ride	tile	wise
life	Mike	pipe

Then the irregular material, but systematically:

owl	fowl	town
sow	cow	towel

ouch	out	pound
loud	round	count

Fifth, the influence of modern grammar on the analysis and appreciation of literature has been significant. In the main, linguistic studies have succeeded in imposing a formal, objective procedure on the analysis of literary forms. Such a procedure is held to be an improvement on impressionistic, subjective approaches to literary form and style, or at the very least, is understood as a viable, complementary adjunct to the more familiar approaches to literature.

There are other areas of instruction that have been influenced by the insights into language that have come from modern structural grammar. But we needn't be detained by them here. We can return to the main line of the discussion—the teaching of structural grammar in the schools. This is the primary application of the science of structural linguistics. The secondary matters of the applications to teaching composition and literature will be treated in full in the next chapter.

Structural Grammar in the English Curriculum

Among the more interesting applications of the teaching of phonology have been (1) the analysis of English intonation and (2) the teaching of dialectology.

For the first case, the reader will recall from Chapter Three that English has pitch, stress, and juncture. This systematic, deep-seated, structural device is something children have great fun learning about. We can look at one investigation that students are conducting into intonation. They collect short phrases like

1. a dancing teacher
2. a reading assignment
3. a listening device
4. an eating place
5. a crying towel
6. his flying lessons

The students then mark the intonational features for each phrase:

1a.   a   dán   cing teàcher

2a.   a   réad   ing assìgnment

3a.   a   lísten   ing devìce

Note: The raised and lowered parts of words indicate high and low pitches.

4a.   an   éat   ing plàce

5a.   a   crý   ing tòwel

6a.   his   flý   ing lèssons

For these grammatically similar structures, the student discovers a consistent intonational pattern: strong stress to weaker stress and high to low pitch sequence. He also finds, if he is diligent, that only one of the six phrases can be said with a different tune, namely

1b.   a dâncing   téach   er

1a speaks of a teacher of dancing. 1b speaks of a teacher who is dancing.

The student notes that

6b.   his flying   lés   sons

can only apply to papers and notes sent hurtling through the air, but that

4b.   an eating   plá   ce

has no imaginable context except as a feeble joke about a place that eats.

This kind of investigation can be carried out through innumerable such structures. Let's look at a few more.

7. library card
8. a house party
9. a press release
10. an English sentence
11. a city planner
12. a precision instrument

The intonation features are as follows:

```
                    lí
7a.    a
                  brary càrd

                  hóuse
8a.    a
                          pàrty

                préss
9a.    a
                      releàse

                              sént
10a.   an  Ênglish
                                  ence

                        plán
11a.   a    cîty
                            ner

                              ín
12a.   a    precision
                            strument
```

All six of these phrases have the same surface structure: *article + noun + noun*. But examples 7 through 9 have a falling pitch sequence, whereas examples 10 through 12 have a rising pitch sequence. The student is diving and delving in the wonders of English phonology. He usually comes through it better informed, if giddy.

Another investigation that sheds much light on the workings of English phonology begins with the gathering of short sentences like the following:

```
                      met
13.   You haven't
                          him.

                      met  him?
14.   You haven't

                         m
15.   Who did you         e
                            e
                             t?
```

With these three sentences, the students can learn that there are two intonational patterns that are associated with statements and questions. All statements are spoken with mid-to-high-to-low pitches; all questions that begin with *who, what, why*, etc. are spoken with the *same* pitch sequence. (Compare examples 13 and 15.) But questions like number 14, that is, questions that have the so-called regular syntax, have the pitch sequence mid-to-high. Meanwhile,

16. Did you ^{meet him?}

16. Did you $^{\text{meet him?}}$

which has so-called reverse syntax, has the mid-to-high sequence, too.

Now look at the following brief conversation:

He: He married my ^{sis} ter.

She: ^{Wh}o?

He: ^{Char} lie.

She: $^{\text{N}}_{\text{o.}}$ I mean which ^{sis} ter?

He: $^{\text{O}}_{\text{h.}}$ Thel $_{\text{ma.}}$

She: $_{\text{W}}$h$^{\text{o?}}$

He: ^{Thel} ma.

When *She* first asks "Who" *He* doesn't know if *She* is looking for a man's name or a woman's. As it turns out, *She* was interested in knowing which sister it was who had been married. When *She* learns that it was Thelma, *She* doesn't believe it. *She* expresses her disbelief by the way *she* says "who" the second time, low-to-mid-to-high. Then, since *He* is saying "Thelma" for the second time, *He* goes from very high-to-low rather than from high-to-low.

Once again, students are after the facts. Needless to say, the materials presented above do not exhaust the possibilities for this area of instruction and learning. It is quite possible to develop materials of this kind that can be investigated over several weeks, even months, of the school year. And that's exactly what is being done. The important points that need to be stressed are: first, that these attributes of English are fundamental features of the language and are therefore deserving of inquiry on the part of students, and second, that the facts needn't be spooned into students, but rather, that students can be encouraged to ask the right questions and then to proceed to find workable answers. Then too, a lesson on English intonation must be very carefully structured in the English curriculum: it is not a matter for random or coincidental investigation.

We move on to the second example of an application of the study of phonology—dialect geography. It is true that the various dialects of English are distinguished on more than phonological grounds. But we can successfully discuss both dialect geography and its application to the schoolroom while confining the discussion to the phonological level.

The first thing that can be learned is the techniques of dialect geography. One way to do this is to present the facts of the case. The inductive method is perhaps better suited to this particular case, however. The mobility of our people makes it a virtual certainty that even young children in classrooms will have come from divergent dialectal backgrounds. It is not at all uncommon for an eight- or ten-year-old student to have lived in three or four different parts of the country. With a situation like this, any English teacher who prevented his students from investigating speech differences that they hear every day ought to consider seriously getting into some other line of work. It would be like a biology teacher who, faced with clamorous youngsters who have just discovered an ant colony in the corner of the room, tells his class that today they are going to read about microscopes and that he will get the janitor to take care of the ants.

There are different kinds of dialect divergences. One sort arises for essentially geographical reasons, another for social reasons. The first recognizes the linguistic reflexes of the geographical distribution of people. The second attends to various differences in speech that have come about through social stratification. It comes as a surprise to many, but nonetheless, the language that the first English-speaking settlers spoke in and around Boston, Providence, Richmond, and Charleston was the language that they brought with them from the various counties of England. Since these settlers had been cut off from immediate and direct discourse with the people left behind and found in the New World strange things that needed naming, it was quite natural that the English they spoke in the colonies should become different from Island English. Similarly, the early cultural centers that arose were cut off from one another, so further differences came about. Then, with the westward movement, the climate for change intensified as inland centers became established in Pittsburgh, Detroit, Chicago, St. Louis, and other places. Each developed its soci-cultural, linguistic norms and radiated its influence to the neighboring areas. All of this is an extremely brief account of only a few of the factors that were at work, but it will serve as a backdrop against which we can examine some investigations that students can profitably propose and follow through.

On the phonological level, which happens to be the ones we are exemplifying, the most fertile ground for inquiry is among the notorious hallmarks of phonologically based dialectal differences, the "dropped-r" speech of Eastern New England, for instance, or the "clipped-nasal" speech of Chicago, or the "drawl" of Southern speech. Any one of these will serve nicely as a way for a teacher and his students to begin learning something new about their language.

Take New England speech. If a class in Chicago is lucky enough to have a newcomer from Boston, a first-hand "informant" will liven things up considerably. In the absence of a youthful Bostonian, careful monitoring in Chicago of national television and radio programs will have to do. Of course if we begin in a Boston classroom, the students will be mystified by any talk of a peculiar "dropped-r" speech, or at least many of them will. Attention is always drawn to someone who "speaks with an accent"—the other guy. "What, me, speak with an accent?" "Everybody talks funny but me!"

The child from Boston may very well have few differences in his speech from the speech of the Chicago children, and one of them may not be "r-less" speech. Such speech has become pretty much a relic. I heard a good Eastern New England mother shout at her son, "Get out of the cah, Bawby!" Bobby's sister shouted back, "Bobby's not in the car, mother." Part of the explanation for this may be that the children had heard as much English from the television set, maybe more, as they had heard from their father and mother.

But the Chicago youngsters will detect some differences between their speech and the Boston lad's. If he says *cah*, he will also say /stoh/ for *store*, /puh/ for *poor*, /iyh/ for *ear*, and so forth. He will pronounce *aunt* and *bath* with a vowel somewhere between the /a/ of *father* and the /æ/ of *cat*. His *darn* and *Don* will sound alike. Conversely, to his ear, his new friends will pronounce *cat* and *can't* alike*; occasional their *dese* and *dose* for *these* and *those* will sound odd. And so on back and forth until everyone is satisfied that he has noted all the differences including incidental ones that lack pattern, one of which is the hopeless mess concerning the pronunciation of the two cities. The Boston boy himself will sometimes say *Bahston* but other times *Bawston*. And the Chicago kids will say both *Chicahgo* and *Chicawgo*. To make matters words, one kid in the front row will turn up saying *Tchicago*.

Neil Postman in his book *Linguistics: A Revolution in Teaching* reports what happened to a class in Massachusetts that made the mistake of asking itself "Did the characters in Mark Twain's *Huck Finn* really talk that way?" After the class cleared up what they meant by "the characters" and "that way," they found themselves preparing a comprehensive questionnaire that they sent to their counterparts in Hannibal, Missouri, for taped responses. Along the way they designed a method to translate the written words into a suitable form, did the necessary research in the library, and formulated precise, answerable questions like "Do the . . . speech characteristics of Huck Finn represented in Mark Twain's novel still appear in the dialect of boys thirteen to fifteen years of age in the area of Hannibal, Missouri?" *They found a subject for investigation. They clarified the problem. They went to work.*

What all this shows is that dialect geography is not only something that can be taught. It is something that can be *learned*. What is more, it is something that can be *done*. In this, students are not receptacles into which is poured the knowledge of the ages. In the absence of other things worth doing in the classroom, this kind of thing—pouring information down gullets—can be a last resort before

---

*Archibald Hill reports that a Chicago youth wrote "I mint have done it better" which shows, considering the spelling of 'might' (*mint*), from the inadvertent spelling that nasality is at work in the student's speech (to an extent that is probably not common elsewhere.)

the utter cynicism of engaging students in truly wasteful projects. But students can be allowed to *discover* knowledge. If the teacher already knows what the answers are, he can make sure that the direction the students' probings are taking them will lead to previously established truths, being careful to remember that blind alleys and wrong answers are not necessarily to be avoided. Indeed, often as not, wrong answers are useful in the learning process. Experience and history instruct us severely on this point. One of the instructions is that hard-won answers are the only ones worth asking questions about. The familiar story of Thomas Edison's invention of the electric light will serve us here. To put it mildly, Edison didn't succeed in his first try. Between first idea and first tentative success lay the enormous frustration of good questions and lousy answers.

Now we can move on to *morphology* in this brief overview of grammar in the classroom.

In Dringby Town

In Dringby town by the creeling Og
I wroned my conspicular shirps—
Eekless, furpish, and aslade
I whimmied the urgled thirps.

But when her lighs in faneful lonce
Did adane my sorden feal—
Fallonly, solenly, I underclecked
My nonconstipulent weel.

Here is a poem that has no chance of being anthologized. But it is the kind of thing that can be used very well in the detection of regular morphological signals in English. Look at it again, this time with some parts missing.

In Dringby Town

In _____ _____ by the ____-ing __
I ____-d my _____-ar ____-s—
___-less, ____-ish, and a- _____
I _____-ed the __-ed _____-s.

But when her __-s in ____-ful _____
Did _____ my __-en ____ —
_____-ly, ____-ly, I under-_____-ed
My non-_____-ent ____.

The language of this poem communicates its "messages" without the benefit of nouns, verbs, adjectives, and adverbs *that we recognize.* Students can see that grammatical categories are based on something more tangible than "name of a person, place, or thing" or "word that expresses action." Students can discover the structural attributes of word classes in English. It's ironic that nonsense should be the vehicle for illuminating these structural forms, for after all, isn't it meanings of words that give sentences their meaning? The answer is neither yes or no. The answer is that the meaning of a sentence is in part due to the meanings of the words. This suggests that there is something else that contributes to meaning. That something else is syntax. And syntax is form. *Form underlines meaning.* The nonsense poem points up the fact that this is so.

> . . . I underclecked
>
> My nonconstipulent weel.

The form of this sentence is signalled by (1) the *shape* of the words in it and (2) the relationship of the words, one to another. Compare

> . . . I underestimated
>
> My inconspicuous friend.

This real English sentence has the same syntactic *form* as the line from the poem. It happens that the line from the poem has only two real English words out of five, while the sentence above has five out of five.

Beginning here, or at a similar point, the English teacher can get his students to discover exactly what such formal properties of English sentences are. They can detect the "traffic cops" of English sentences, forms like *the, my, her; in, at; do, did, has; and, but;* and so forth, as in

> *But* when *her* lighs *in* faneful lonce
> *Did* adane *my* sodden feal—

They can learn to identify the formal properties of adjectives and adjectivals and some other things by charting their inflectional behavior and by plotting their distributional characteristics:

> In *Dringby* town by the *creel* |ing| Og
> I wroned my *conspicul* |ar| shirps —
> *Eek* |less,| *furp* |ish,| and |a| *slade*
> I whimmied the *urgl* |ed| thirps.

They can discover what a verb is by noting its unique inflectional-distributional behavior.

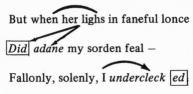

But when her lighs in faneful lonce

$\boxed{Did}$ *adane* my sorden feal –

Fallonly, solenly, I *undercleck* $\boxed{ed}$

My nonconstipulent weel.

These matters learned in an orderly fashion and across the broadest possible base can serve students well in their quest for knowledge of the *internal structure and form* of the English language. What is interesting about it all is that results of their investigations show not much more than a naming of knowledge that they have mastered long before they ever came to talk about what they know. As far as their knowledge of the *form* of English is concerned, they know perfectly well what "nouns, verbs, and adjectives" are, even though they have never heard these words. All normal kindergarten children know what the forms are of the sentences they say and hear. They will not say any of the odd-numbered sentences below, but they would and do say sentences like the even-numbered ones.

1. *Seven littled white kittens.
2. I can't find my poor little old broken truck.
3. *He to used be my friendly.
4. I'll tell you if you keep it a secret.
5. *Why don't you go her ask for it?
6. Under the dresser by the closet in Tommy's room.

They will not say any of the odd-numbered sentences because they know that the *form* of English does not permit them. They will say the even-numbered ones because they know that the "inflections," the "derivational affixes," and the "syntax" are O.K.

The last illustration of modern grammar using structural techniques to develop lessons is in syntax proper. Here are some phrases:

1. Some . . . . .men
2. Some . . . . space men
3. Some . . . . green space men
4. Some . . . . . . little green space men

5.   ..... funny little green space men
6.   Some funny little green space men

A collection of phrases like these will suggest that there are *order classes* of adjectives. We do not say,

7. *Funny some green little space men

Consider a similar set:

8. Any one of the ....cakes
9. Any one of the .... birthday cakes
10. Any one of the .... chocolate birthday cakes
11. Any one of the .... large chocolate birthday cakes
12. Any one of the .....very large chocolate birthday cakes
13.   ....mother's very large chocolate birthday cakes
14. Any one of mother's very large chocolate birthday cakes

If you and I had the patience, we could enumerate a sufficient number of such sets of phrases to identify with some precision the order classes that adjectives (and some other things) fall into in their patterning before nouns in noun-phrase constructions. But you and I are too old. Let's leave it to the kids who have heaps of patience. What they find out when they do the work is that all such noun phrases display a regular internal ordering of the items that comprise the sets. Having identified their order classes, they can approach a given phrase, say,

15. All of Douglas's pretty beat-up old baseball bats

and analyze it as having an ordering of forms.

One can go about this business in a slightly different way by listing strings of words like the following:

16. *my books all school new
17. *Susie's dresses pretty pastel-colored new sun
18. *all-transistor his receiver set stereo
19. *the backyard Laramie's second sale annual

Then turn the kids loose on them. They will not only unfailingly reorder the terms of such phrases; they may be persuaded by what they have been able to do (since they know so much) that this knowledge should be in the forefront of their minds whenever they speak or write. It is perfectly possible for someone to get things out of order and thereby *inadvertently* (That's a terrible word!) bring about a breakdown in communication. A student of mine once wrote " ... his early familiar style" when the context called for

" . . . his familiar early style." The two are quite different. An alertness to the trap that the language had set for him might have helped him avoid writing a phrase he didn't want.

The matter of "structural ambiguity" can also be confronted intelligently by learning the rules of English sentence construction.

20. Did you see that woman on the chair with the funny feet?
21. He has never been sent there with my approval.
22. There is an echo in the valley that never ends.
23. She does what I do well.
24. He shot the man with hate in his eyes.
25. People who drive while drinking sometimes end up dead.

Each of these sentences says two things instead of one. The structural signals in the sentences are not clear. Take sentence 24 for example. This sentence may mean either that the man who was shot had hate in his eyes or that the man who did the shooting had hate in his eyes. The crucial structural point is that the prepositional phrase *with hate in his eyes* may be serving either an adverbial function (shot . . . *with hate in his eyes*) or an adjectival function (the man *with hate in his eyes*). The other sentences are similarly fouled up. And it is surprising how much of this there is in English speech and writing. There needn't be (except for special effects, comic maybe).

These few examples of classroom work based on modern structural grammar will suggest the possibilities for instruction. Needless to say, there is system and complexity at every turn in English; thus the structure of the native tongue can be confronted directly, and students can learn much from the confrontation. Their native faculty for inquisitiveness and their inborn powers of doubt can be married to the scientific method that is the hallmark of structural grammar. As may have been sensed from the presentation, not much is left to chance; nor are preconceptions permitted to interfere with an objective analysis based on gathering, classification, and verification; nor, indeed, is any answer ever accepted as final. This may sound unduly scientific. What, after all, is science doing in an English classroom? In the opinion of this author, it's high time that linguistic science got into the classroom and cleared out some of the impressionistic, opinion-based muck that has passed for the "good news" about the English language and its use. (There is a danger of carrying science too far. Science doesn't have much to say about poetry or the affairs of the heart, but it has *some* things to say about *some* poetry!) When we still find teachers who hang signs that say I SAY AIN'T around the necks of eight-year-olds, we must admit that such teachers have reached their highest level of incompetence. Is it our purpose in education to be accusatory and intimidating of children? I think not. If I am wrong and the teachers who do such things are right—if this isn't the grossest example of the kind of insult that can be heaped on children—then the purpose of education is for teachers to determine what "acceptable" behavior is and see to it that everybody conforms, which, according to my understanding of words, constitutes an élite totalitarianism. If we espouse diversity and freedom while abhorring conformity and servility, our only just course is not only to permit children to find their own truths but to insist that they do.

But I have allowed my convictions to get the better of me. (Sometime let me tell you what I think of punishing children for running in the halls by making them *write* five hundred times that they won't. Someday, somewhere, somebody is going to punish a child for running in the halls by making him run around the track five hundred times. *That* would place gym in its proper perspective and let writing off the hook.)

Transformational Grammar in the Classroom

It is becoming increasingly more clear that the abstract theory of transformational-generative grammar can find no place in the classroom. More specifically, there is little value or justification in trying to make theoretical grammarians out of kids in school. There is much worth in leading students to basic understandings of language, however. The fallout from the explosion of knowledge, if it is constituted properly, is more like manna than a radioactive cloud. What *can* be done with the ideas of transformational grammar follows, with some of the details translated into childrenese.

First, conscious awareness of the basic syntactic structures that undergird English sentences leads logically to a thoughtful, informed control of these patterns. A teacher can bring his students to this awareness by getting them to recognize what are called *kernel sentences.*

1. The man is my friend (now).
2. The man is here (now).
3. The man is old (now).
4 The man is in the park (now).
5. The man sees my friend now).
6. The man laughs (now).

Students can then produce variations on these patterns:

7. A woman is our teacher.
8. My sister was home yesterday.
9. That girl is pretty.
10. My pencils are in my pocket.
11. Her dog ate the bone.
12. Most women cry.

From here, learning about English can go in many directions. *Transformations* can be introduced immediately and effectively, as follows:

1a. Is the man my friend?
2a. Is the man here?
3a. Is the man old?
4a. Is the man in the park?
5a. Does the man see my friend?
6a. Does the man laugh?

Let me stress that even though in this short space I have introduced two elements of transformational grammar that can be taught to children, we can by no means assume that both kernel sentences and transformations can be taught in a short period. These are not topics for a week's lesson, or a month's, or even a year's. These are topics that can be introduced simply at first, but with extreme care, with progressively greater complexity as time goes on, again with care, and in great detail in the later grades.

A third, and vitally important, insight from transformational grammar, namely, *embedding*, plays a crucial role in any truly modern program of studies. Embedding is the process of containing one structure within another. If kernel sentences are irreducible (cannot be made any smaller), then non-kernel sentences are reducible. By embedding the kernel sentence

13. She is pretty.

in the kernel sentence

14. She is a lady.

we get the non-kernel sentence

15. She is a pretty lady.

To put the matter differently, if we begin with sentence 15, we can "trace its history" to sentences 13 and 14. This view of how English works is of incalculable value. It has all sorts of applications, not the least of which is in composition. Some will say that there is nothing new here, that children have been doing this for years in school. Not by a long shot! What they have been doing is tinkering with simple sentences trying to make them complicated. It has been a hit-or-miss business lacking comprehensiveness and rigor. The lesson is not so simple as presenting students with a half-dozen simple sentences and asking them to "subordinate them properly."

Embedding is extremely complicated. It cannot be understood from general directions and vague admonitions. It can only be understood after a most careful, ordered, and thorough analysis. But the rewards are great because students who have mastered the process are in a position to manage the composition of their ideas with variety and precision, sometimes even with grace. It is taken as axiomatic that competent writing results from the thoughtful selection and arrangement of the sound-sense signals of the language. Variety and precision, ladies and gentlemen, *is* embedding.

Kernel, transformation, embedding—these are three dandies for English programs.

It should be stressed that one of the widely recognized weaknesses in much English instruction has come from the fragmentation of the concerns of English. "On Monday, we shall write a composition. On Tuesday, we shall complete our grammar lesson. Then on Wednesday and Thursday, we shall discuss the poem on page 278. Friday, as usual, we shall have our spelling test." We can safely be scornful of a program like that.

It is probably not possible to learn about grammar, composition, reading, and literature all at the same time. But a reasonable articulation of all the concerns of English should be undertaken. At the very least, students should sense that what they did last week is related somehow to what they are doing this week.

Be this as it may, very many aspects of how the English language works *grammatically* can be, and are being, taught children and adolescents from the transformational-generative point of view. One lesson ties in some literature. Look at Edwin Arlington Robinson's poem "Richard Cory."

Richard Cory

Whenever Richard Cory went down town,
We people on the pavement looked at him.
He was a gentleman from sole to crown,
Clean favored, and imperially slim.

And he was always quietly arrayed,
And he was always human when he talked;
But still he fluttered pulses when he said,
"Good-morning," and he glittered when he walked.

And he was rich — yes, richer than a king —
And admirably schooled in every grace:
In fine, we thought that he was everything
To make us wish that we were in his place.

So on we worked, and waited for the light,
And went without the meat, and cursed the bread;
And Richard Cory, one calm summer night,
Went home and put a bullet through his head.

Teachers and students could spend a very long time on the wonders of this poem. They could (and should) exhaust themselves over it.

After they have noted the rhyme scheme, and after they have decided what the poem *means*—that rich people sometimes commit suicide because money doesn't buy happiness (which would come as a surprise to a student I heard about who thought that the poem was about the Communist scourge)—in other words, after they have dispensed with the trivialities, they can look around for more telling commentary. For one thing, they may find that there are eleven *and*'s in the poem. Add to these the *but*, the *in fine*, and the *so*, and we have fourteen "linkers," almost one per line, enough to make almost any old-style English teacher cringe. The processes of conjunction-subordination are a formidable component of the poem. Phrases of less than sentence size are conjoined (eleven times) in the larger sentences. They are *embedded*.

> 1. Richard Cory went down town.
> 2. People looked at him.
> 3. People were on the pavement.
> 4. We were the people.

are the sources for

> (Whenever) Richard Cory went down town,
> We people on the pavement looked at him.

Similarly,

> 5. He was quietly arrayed.
> 6. He was always human.
> 7. He talked.
> 8. Still, he fluttered pulses.
> 9. He said something (i.e., "Good-morning").
> 10. He glittered.
> 11. He walked.

are the sources for

> And he was always quietly arrayed,
> And he was always human when he talked;
> But still he fluttered pulses when he said,
> "Good-morning," and he glittered when he walked.

And so on, discovering the *history* of Robinson's lines. The lines are of an imposing and integral simplicity. But look where we have led ourselves—to a fairly obvious conclusion: that the grammar of the poem is perfectly tuned to at least one of the sensibilities of the poem. The childlike awe before Richard Cory on the part of the people is mirrored in the "childlike" language. How apt it is that the public voice of the poem should align simple thoughts simply!

Let's take one more step into the poem, this time with a very soft tread. There are, it seems to me, three stunning phrases in the poem, not counting the real zinger in the last stanza, "And went without the meat, and cursed the bread." The expressions that I have in mind are

> 1. imperially slim
> 2. he fluttered pulses
> 3. he glittered when he walked

In preparation for this discussion it was mentioned that an adequate grammar of English could, theoretically at least, formalize the semantic processes of the language; we saw that a special kind of dictionary and special rules could be established to judge sentences as ambiguous or anomalous. Whether this can or cannot be done is not important here. We can most certainly *informally* examine the three phrases for ambiguity and anomaly. There is something mildly anomalous about all three phrases. One can be both *imperial* and *slim*. But how about being *imperially slim*? Of course, we are now in the bedrock of what poetry *is*—fresh ideas. The poet distills experience and demands that the language he controls give up novel expressions for his insights and feelings. And what a fine marriage of ideas we have in this slightly anomalous phrase, *imperially slim*! An empire is a domain of a government that extends over other states; to be *imperial* is to be *of the empire, magisterial, lordly, proud*. Now Robinson takes these two complex notions and marries them to *slimness*. Then, *slim* feeds back into *empire*. Together, they conspire to characterize Richard Cory in a way no other two-word combination could.

Essentially the same kind of analysis may be made for *he fluttered pulses* and *he glittered when he walked*. The special dictionary will fail to show a path between pronouns that refer to human beings and *flutter*. It will show such a path toward *glitter*. But we sense that this sentence about glittering while walking does not relate to the only context that we will accept for it, namely, when we understand that the person's clothes have sequins or bits of glass. Meanwhile, we sense that pulses do indeed flutter, as when someone is very sick. But these are not pulses that are fluttering; this is Richard Cory who is fluttering pulses.

What we have just said is that the insights into language that come from a consideration of transformational grammar can inform our understanding of a poetic technique. Here, anomaly has been identified as a poetic technique in some of the lines in the poem. (Anomaly is "grammatical", incidentally.)

Now I suggest that these two approaches to "Richard Cory" (and by example, to literature) are sound. They are based on respectable, analytical premises. The one gets us going on an analysis of the grammar itself, the other on the meaning(s). A cogent theory of grammar can provide not only the wherewithal but also the stimulus for a provocative, useful approach to language. Such is the kind of theory that is being taught children—*that children are learning*— and such is the variety of investigation that is being conducted by teachers and students for both their sakes.

5

LITERATURE

COMPOSITION ◁————▷ READING

I know I am solid and sound.
To me the converging objects of the universe perpetually flow,
All are written to me, and I must get what the writing means.

WALT WHITMAN, "Song of Myself"

The preceding two chapters have emphasized grammar. It should be clear that grammar in the schools these days is unlike the "grammar" of old. Grammar now has as its main purpose the acquisition of knowledge of how language works. Teaching grammar with this in mind has meant that the messages we get from poets and novelists, essayists and biographers, films, magazines, newspapers, and all the rest are of special interest. The grammar of a poem or a novel is all that the piece is—all that the poem is, all that the novel is. Tone and diction, character and situation, plot and theme are all grammatical. So are the purposes and meanings. Thus, before arriving at this part of the discussion, we suggested very strongly what The New English is all about vis-à-vis literature and reading. But composition, too, you see, is a lesson in modern grammar. Here, the student is on the encoding end of message-making. In either case, two things are true: the student is learning how messages are encoded and decoded; he is learning how a particular message, his own if he is writing, someone else's if he is reading, is encoded or decoded as the case may be. All three things, then—literature, reading, and composition—become a unified set of experiences in the overall curriculum of English instruction. This philosophy of English instruction provides an extremely important coherence for the program. Nearly all matters can now be brought into sharp focus. An English program that lacks coherence and unification is recognized as a weak one, recognition of the weakness leads to correction of the weakness, and correction amounts to a unified *articulation* of the many "subjects" of English.

There is a widely recognized priority scale for these subjects. First comes grammar in the modern sense. After that, in descending order, are literature, reading, composition, and spelling. Some place literature first. Literature is "quintessentially our subject." Maybe so. But priorities are not that important. It helps to have something pretty clearly in mind in this area, but to be bound to one or the other priority scale would be foolish. The highest priority of all, of course, is the learning about language by children and youth. Whether this learning should flow from grammar first and then literature or the other way around really matters little. It's the learning that matters. And *what* is learned matters the most. In fact, it is best to think of The New English as a spiraling upward to linguistic finesse rather than a priorities scheme of relatively important concerns.

The discussion of the new teaching of literature, reading, and composition will necessarily be rather general. We have seen several new techniques for the teaching of literature and language in preceding chapters. We will see a few more here. But it will not be necessary or even useful to lay out all the new modes of instruction in the three topics that make up the subject of this chapter. Indeed, it wouldn't be possible to do so. We will have to content ourselves, as I have just said, with some general suggestions. The occasional detailed discussion will hopefully clarify the main thrusts of the new instruction.

Literature

We can begin with an outline of the rationale for the teaching of literature.

(1)   Until fairly recently, the literature that was taught children never got closer than a generation removed from their time, and even then it was usually a matter of "safe" works taught to high-school seniors. Today, contemporary pieces of literature are being read and discussed by children in school. (It is still true that older students see more of this than younger ones, but the younger ones *are* meeting more meaningful literature.) The high-schoolers are confronting themselves with Agee's *A Death in the Family,* Green's *A Burnt-out Case,* Salinger's *The Catcher in the Rye,* Heller's *Catch 22,* Gover's *One Hundred Dollar Misunderstanding,* and Kesey's *One Flew Over the Cuckoo's Nest.* In some cases, they are reading things that they themselves have selected, for example, *Poems For Pleasure,* which is a collection of poems that tenth and eleventh graders edited.

Now everyone knows that reading such literature as this is a troublesome and worrisome business to students, teachers, and administrators. More than once, the wrath of an irate parent has been visited upon a school when his son or daughter has been asked by a teacher to read this or that "controversial" book. Good, I say. If the teacher in his wisdom wants to teach controversy, or more to the point, if he wants to teach what he feels is suitable literature, then it is his duty to do so. If the parent wants to censor his child's reading, or if he wants to make his voice heard in the classroom, he should do so. At least everybody is interested in what's going on at school. *That* would be a change for the good.

(2)   The broadening of the scope of literary offerings runs upward beyond inclusion of comtemporary literature. The basic idea of literature itself has been redefined to include more than the printed word. Literature need not be books. The literature of the movie house and the television set has been brought into the arena, to say nothing of the principal audio-visual aid of the English classroom, the film. Instead of reading *Romeo and Juliet,* students can *see* it. Instead of an assignment to read the play on page 292, students are sent home to watch the Hallmark or the Xerox show on television. But the broadening of the scope is even more dramatic. It is not only masterworks old and new that students are dealing with. It is the good, the bad, and the indifferent as well. One way to learn something about mediocrity is to study it.

In the past, students had a devil of a time judging literary merit.

Somehow it was never possible for them to determine that a soap opera or a popular nighttime adventure was "bad" literature or that an expensive "special," put on at eight o'clock and ballyhooed all over the place, was merely *Secret Love* moved up from two in the afternoon. Sentiment is not sentimentality. Human rage is not accompanied by an organ. Dramatic conflict is not stereotypical or petty. Character is not "a crooked smile." Meaningfulness in literature is determinable, discoverable. It has basic elements that make it recognizable. And after all, school is just as much a place that prepares students to use their learning as it is a place where students learn things. They can very well learn that *Romeo and Juliet* is a great piece of literature. But if they are not prepared to judge that *King Lear* is also great, then what has been the use?

The inclusion of all kinds of "messages"—good as well as bad—has done nothing to the idea that a prime function of any English program is to teach the masterworks of our heritage. The Beowulf, Chaucer, Shakespeare, Milton, Wordsworth, James, Hemingway— they are all there. But so are the lesser lights and the no-lights-at-all. There has always been more bad literature than good. Preparation for the judging of both is an important part of The New English.

(3)   We repeat here two of the observations that were made in the first couple of paragraphs of this chapter. First, a piece of literature is understood as a linguistic act. Second, literature is a part of an overall program of studies, not a thing apart.

Whatever is taught as literature, classic or latest best seller, printed play or "drama" on TV, the thing itself is a complex linguistic act. If it is viewed at first hand, then it is at once oral and visual. If it is read, it is neither of these. Students who read plays are doubly disadvantaged in that they can neither hear the players nor see them act out their lives. They must go from printed page to the real thing by way of their imaginations. They must "hear" the voices and "see" the action, the sets, the costumes, and the lighting. In this, it is obvious that they do not have the advantage of being witness to the event. Reading a Tennessee Williams play is a more difficult, more demanding job, therefore, than witnessing one of his plays. But as everybody knows, this is a two-way street. There is a lovely advantage to being a mere reader of literature. It allows the imagination full rein. The reader, in going from printed page to a real drama, can hardly expect to get there without putting his imagination in gear. Having engaged it, he finds to his delight that the play is as much his own creation as it is the playwright's. He supplies the voice, the action, and the setting.

Literature, whether it is experienced directly in a theater or at a poetry recitation or indirectly through the medium of the printed page, is not a dismembered and lifeless thing cut off from the other parts of students' linguistic-cultural worlds. As has already been said, literature is an occasion for appreciation and enjoyment, but also for composition or discussion as well as a "grammar lesson."

(4)   Literature is approached for what it is, not for what it is "about." Preparing youngsters for a reading of Robinson's "Richard Cory" does not include lectures on capitalism, creature comforts, envy, suicide, morals, happiness, or prosody. "Richard Cory" *is*! It is not *about*. Literature has an existence of its own (whether it is incorporated in an English program or not). It has an interior design and substance which exist *in vacuo*. It adheres to no other rules than its own. The New English brings students *into* literature, into the special linguistic world that is literature.

(5)   As to the "about," no one doubts that literature carries messages. It is about something or other. But literature doesn't necessarily have a moral. It doesn't necessarily teach a lesson every time out. Let's be blunt: it *rarely* teaches lessons. Very few authors of repute report that they wrote to instruct. Fewer still have expressed any confidence in the proposition that their works have improved man's lot in that they have made him more moral. Even so, all works of literature have one thing in common. They come from a passion. Lewis Carroll wrote passionately for a young girl. Dostoevski wrote passionately for an editor who was three books ahead of him. Hemingway wrote passionately of himself. Faulkner wrote passionately of a reconstructed never-never land. For some the passion has been a sometime thing, for others it has been an "exquisite affliction"; for others, a dark drive toward suicide; for still others, a drawled exhaustion after a completed myth. But, always, the passion.

(I have learned many things as a teacher of youth, one of the most important being that one's own enthusiasm for literature is more influential on students than all the erudite analyses in the world. Once a student sees that that person standing in front of him is *in love* with literature, he is done for. He has been had. Of course, one is not in love with all literature. But when a poet moves you, and you can't hide the fact that he has, the poet's passion and yours get through to the student. I cannot believe, really, that anybody took very seriously Theodore Roethke's parting gesture to his students when he said, "The cage is open. You are free to go." I'll just bet they were! His poetry was passionate. Could his teachings have been otherwise? Were his students "free to go" unmarked? Passion is too real, too intimate, too alive to be dealt with as one deals with a lesson or a lecture.)

A poem given life by passion and experienced by the reader passionately is "about" something. It is about suicide or daffodils or a wasteland or lost youth. But a student must *not* be told in advance what a poem is about. If he is, the game is up. There is nothing left for him to do. He now "knows" what it's about. (Why ever should he read it? He shouldn't! Leave what poems are about to authorities like teachers. What does he know?) Poetry is lost to him forever, or at least until such time as he can again discover it rough-hewn, in its natural state—a private spot for two, the poet and his voice on one side, the ears, heart, and the mind of someone listening on the other.

(6) In a related way, the teaching of literature these days is less a process that transfers the knowledge and opinions of the teacher to the student than it is the birth and maturation of a literary sensibility within students. This is not to say that what teachers know and what teachers think about what they know have no value for students. After all, teaching remains pretty much a matter of guidance, in the best sense of the word, and much in our tradition depends upon guiding children toward and through their literary heritage. But in achieving this, there has been a subtle but profound change in emphasis. We are no longer sure at all what or how literature "means." The inescapable fact is that the same piece of literature will be experienced in as many different ways as there are those who read it. We all bring disparate linguistic-cultural experiences to the separate moments in our lives when we encounter a piece of literature. Of course, it is clear that *Macbeth* is not a garden party. (Neither is Katharine Mansfield's "Garden Party," for that matter.) But there is a vast middle ground for meanings. *Macbeth* has

a middle ground of ambition, intrigue, and murder. But these are topical headings. One man's ambition is another's envy. One man's envy is another's ruthlessness. And is it Macbeth's ambition or his wife's? What about the witches? How do they fit in? Is Macbeth mad? Is Macduff's rage understandable? How? What do we know about Macbeth that Macduff doesn't? Does what we know about Macbeth matter in our final judgment of him? These are all questions that a teacher can properly ask. If the students do not ask them, the teacher *must*. But answer them with only the greatest care. Doctrinaire, authoritarian answers are wrong. There are never any final answers in literature or criticism, and even if there were, they would be of only modest value to students. Whenever answers to literary questions are given, they should be given in the context of developing the critical faculties of students. They need intelligent guidance, not indoctrination on what a piece of literature "means."

(7) Despite these points, there are some things in literature that are left to "local control." National goals do not presuppose a national program in the sense that every fifteen-year-old in the land is reading the same book on the same day. Students have different backgrounds, interests, and abilities. The idea of a standardized, uniform program would therefore be a foolish one. That book that challenges a particular group of students at a particular time is the right book for that group. A group, however, is not necessarily a class. As often as not, interest groups form within a class membership, some doing one thing, others doing something else. ("Tracking" is neither all good nor all bad. It is probably more bad than good, though. Placing students into groups according to ability has been less than entirely successful. It's one of those practices that looks better on paper. The unfortunate result, especially in many large metropolitan school districts, is that tracking becomes the unwitting tool of the larger segregation that mars our culture. A child who has begun with an inferior education finds himself shunted to lower and lower tracks. The schools spend less and less on his education and more and more on his friend from "the other side of the track." (How's that for mixing metaphors, Miss Fiditch?) The whole system rises up to guarantee his miseducation. It spends $2.85 on his education and $5.65 on the privileged student's. His teachers are the ones who couldn't make it into Valhalla High out in

Southfield Shores. It even comes to this: when he goes out for the basketball team, he is issued a hand-me-down uniform from Valhalla. But I digress.)

Some English teachers believe that the trouble with low-tracked students is that they have been damned by a middle-class test administered years ago. They believe that the way to teach such students is not to give them watered-down material from the fast class but to confront them with what they have missed, to demand more, not less, to give them their first opportunity to succeed in something. A young Negro who has to have Langston Hughes explained to him by a white man is not a "slow learner." He is a deprived learner. His agony has had no opportunity to be touched by the passion of a Negro poet. He has been systematically excluded from an education. So his teacher's devotion becomes greater, not less. His attention to the students' real needs becomes direct and tangible. Instead of droning on about Wordsworth while the girls stare out from behind a dread of going home and the boys snigger over comic books held deftly over the text page, the New English teacher leaves off his golden daffodils and heads for the heart of the matter—the language of the family in the ghetto, the literature of Batman. Wordsworth's purpose, remember, in his own words, was "to adopt the very language of men." Can a teacher's purpose be otherwise? (Next year, or the next, the teacher can return to Wordsworth, to "The World Is Too Much With Us, Late and Soon," maybe, or "It Is a Beauteous Evening, Calm and Free," or "We Are Seven.")

These seven factors characterize much of what The New Literature is. The program recognizes a broader scope of literature. It deals with it as an instance of language and coordinates it with the other major concerns of English—reading, language (grammar), and composition. It focuses on literature as literature, not on what it is about or on what is called "American Literature" or "British Literature." It demands much less from students in the way of standard answers to standard questions. On the contrary, it recognizes that literature is a private affair. It does not fail to impart the good opinion of the ages, nor does it fail to provide great books for reading. But its main purpose is to bring students into the wide, wide world of "literature" so that they can bring themselves to know its ways, its pertinence, and its delights.

The purposes, then, are threefold: first, to impart the literary part of our heritage, more specifically, to take from our literary heritage that which is pertinent and meaningful to the present generation; second, to open up an ever-widening perspective on life so that students will turn literature on rather than off, having found it savory; and third, to so engage students' hearts and minds in their desire to know themselves, in their need to understand the forces that are at work on them from within and without, that a life without the bittersweet enjoyment of books and films and plays and recitations and magazines would be unthinkable.These are large purposes, grandiose, you might say. Purposes are usually so. Still, they are admirable. There must be some purpose, some *raison d'être*, for any program. The purposes these days are not much different from those that have gone before; nevertheless, the means are so different that we really have quite a different ball game.

Much gobbledygook has been written on purposes and goals, a lot of it from departments of English in schools, even colleges, unfortunately. Beyond its meaningless pomposity, the chief fault of much of it is that *language* has utterly been lost sight of. There is much talk of the "self," citizenship, patriotism, morality, and manners. However virtuous talk on these subjects may be, literature as literature remains selection and combination of the sound-sense elements of language. Without doubt, most people who write poems and novels or make films are people who have something to say on manners and morality, and an obvious benefit that accrues to students who are exposed to such works is that they are trapped into dealing with what has been said. But literature viewed merely as propaganda is literature viewed too narrowly. A legitimate goal of any instruction in our schools is the awakening of the democratic spirit. That spirit is not awakened by vacuous talk about "self" or by indoctrination, certainly not by utterly neglecting language in English classrooms.

"Don't teach anything that is controversial!" What a pernicious imperative that is! To overstate the case, it means that for poetry you teach "moon—June," for biography you teach unforgettable characters, for the film, it's Walt Disney. From the students' point of view, in other words, this is much ado about nothing. An informed sense of responsibility to oneself and to the human race, an independent, critical appreciation of what it means to be alive at the end of the twentieth century, a private moral victory won independently and vitally on the battleground of diverse ideas—these things can never be the product of a "safe," stultifying curriculum. An emphatic affirmation of a pertinent literary heritage, a widening perspective, and a wrestling with one's own humanity—these things characterize the legitimate, if large, purposes of literature in the school.

Composition

Composition has not been so much a calamity as it has been a disaster. Several things have happened in recent years, however, to revitalize and improve instruction and learning in composition. It is the aim of this short section to set forth briefly the major revisions.

No teacher of The New English puts any stock in the idea that training in traditional grammar leads generally and inexorably to good writing. As has been mentioned before, the idea has been tested and proved false many times. Then too, it has come to be accepted that a mechanical approach to writing with its introduction (opening), body (middle), and conclusion (closing) and all the other rhetorical dreariness leads merely to stiff, artificial, strained stuff that would make anyone sleep soundly. (If the old assignment in literature to identify ten metaphors and five similes in a Shakespeare soliloquy did Shakespeare in, the old composition assignment to cast rigorously whatever ideas a student happened to have on a subject in a neat three-part package did the same thing to writing.) We know now that consequential writing follows no model. Competent writing has brightness and *originality*. Great writing *becomes* a model. (I'd better hasten to admit that the argument in the preceding three sentences is illogical. By the time we get to the point about great writing becoming a model, we are back to the thing that was proved wrong in the first sentence where the point was that consequential writing doesn't follow a model. But, you see, Shakespeare as a "model" has never been copied successfully! It is "model" in that sense that was intended above.) This much is painfully true: writing that follows from the prescriptions and proscriptions in handbooks on writing (millions of them!) usually measures up to the standard (model) of the prose in the handbook, that is, grade-A awful. In a word (or four) *you can't write writing.* (Miss Fiditch will have a fit over all the parentheses in this paragraph. I think they're sort of nice.)

More painfully, it is now widely believed that of the forty million children in school, very few should spend much time on writing. Of the carloads of compositions produced daily, there is only a handful worth reading, and these are either from the very young or from the one or two in the senior class for whom the miracle has happened. They can write! If the others haven't brought themselves beyond a minimum competence in writing by the time they are twelve or thirteen, they had better give up. Their linguistic powers are very well fixed by that time. No amount of help will have any effect, especially if their experiences are impoverished. Ten thousand hours drill on topic sentences, paragraphing, development, rhetorical lily gilding, and all the rest are ten thousand hours wasted if the student has no topic.

It makes no difference at all whether compositions and themes are well planned or spontaneous, whether they are marked scrupulously or not at all, whether they are corrected and rewritten or thrown in the waste basket. Innumerable investigations have shown that these tactics have no bearing on improvement. "Correcting" incidentally, as it has been traditionally practiced, has been a gross insinuation of an authoritarian standard, which is a polysyllabic way of saying that it has been petty and stupid. Worse, it has had the opposite result than was intended. It has made students detest writing. We are none of us so old that we can't remember what it was like when we got that beautiful theme back with a C- on it and miles of red ink. It wouldn't have been so bad if the words in red had been mildly encouraging or if they had been about something important. But no. The second paragraph (the one we liked best!) didn't have something called a "topic sentence"; there was no "conclusion"—as if there should have been one (it was implicit in what we said!); and worst of all, the red said "If you're going to write about heroes, Billy, you had better learn how to spell HERO!"

A narrow, authoritarian view of correctness has nothing to do with good writing. Those teachers who used to have the most to say about it knew the least about it. They actually believed that faulty usage was bad grammar. To be less devious, they didn't know the difference between grammar and usage. From an ignorance this profound, all things were possible, including "merit-demerit" systems wherein Johnny could rack up forty or fifty demerits for his contractions, his periodless sentences, and his inevitable misspelled words, while Mary Jane could get heaps of merits for her perfect little circles over all her *i*'s and, in fact, could win the teacher's effulgent adoration for her occasional "I have never journeyed to Chicago but that I have visited the museums."

But this characterization of the world of composition and the people who lived there is depressing, isn't it? This is the way things used to be (it says here). Let's back down a bit and paint a rosier picture. We can do this by looking again at some of the points just made, but in a different light. The first two or three points about the lack of connection between training in traditional grammar and successful writing and about a stiff, rhetorical modeling of writing indicate merely that these specific tactics have no value. A grammar that explicitly sets forth the rules for the enumeration of acceptable sentences as a tactic in writing has already proven to be an aid in composition. More recent rhetorics, too, suggest very strongly that there are some "mechanical" things that can be undertaken as a means to improve writing. We can rightly insist, at the least, that the "mechanics of composition" that we teach remotely resemble some facts about good writing, that they make sense.

There is no doubt at all that the most powerful grammar we have (the one that does the best job of explaining how English works, transformational-generative grammar) should have its rewards in the teaching of composition. So we can pass the point by without laboring it. But what of the more powerful rhetorics? Here we will pause and look.

First, let's characterize "rhetoric" briefly. It is something called the "effective" use of words in speaking and writing. In particular, it is the art or the science that studies such use. Of course, it is *ex post facto:* somebody argues effectively, and the rhetorician follows hard on with his explanation of how the effective argument was achieved. That's rhetoric in a nutshell.

In the main, traditional rhetoric, like school grammar, is fraud-ulent. One of its basic tenets is that principal ideas *must* be cast in main clauses. Supposedly, when you have a complex thought, the main idea goes in the main clause and the subordinate idea or ideas go in subordinated clauses. That sounds perfectly logical, doesn't it? What could be more obvious? Well, for one thing, the nose on your face, if you have one and I am staring at it. What *is* obvious about main ideas in sentences is that they are often off in a corner of the sentence somewhere.

> We turned the corner only to find *that the world*
> *had come to an end.*

> Oh, say can you see, by the dawn's early light,
> What so proudly we hailed at the twilight's last gleaming. . .
> Gave proof through the night *that our flag was still there.*

Since the meat of these sentences is obviously not in the main clauses, the stodgy rhetorician is left with his theory. We may say that there is a *general* validity to the rhetorical principle of main idea in main clause, that as a rule of thumb it works out pretty well, and that children could do worse than to practice the principle. We may say this, but I wouldn't recommend it. Rather, we should examine successful sentences, be fair in statements about how they work, and then if the spirit moves us, try out what we have learned. (I am very heavily indebted to Professor James Sledd's article "Coordination (Faulty) and Subordination (Upside-Down)" for this discussion of the faults of tradition rhetoric. The article originally appeared in the December, 1956, issue of *College Composition and Communication*.)

The new rhetoric, like the new grammar, is much more interested in facts than it is in traditional formulations of the tried and the "true." Not all of the facts that it has found interesting are of interest to us, however. It is the part of the new rhetoric that illuminates the writing processes that we are interested in. Specifically, it is the rhetoric of the paragraph and the composition that needs now to be described. (The ensuing sketch will owe much to the work of Francis Christensen, especially his article "A Generative Rhetoric of the Paragraph," which was published in the October, 1965, issue of *College Composition and Communication*.)

Paragraphs are like human beings. They are all quite different, but they are the "same," too. We have never mistaken a human being for anything else. We will never mistake a paragraph for something else.

For one thing, they are the only things in the world that look like the blotch of black and white that you are staring at. There's mostly white above and mostly white below. In between, there are narrower white spaces above and below rows of black squiggles. Such is this singular thing, the paragraph. (Let's do another one.)

A human being has one body with two legs sticking out from the bottom, two arms from near the top, sideways, and one head. The whole thing has been known to make both love and war, to speak, and to die. The quality of its love-making, war-making, speech, and death differs from one to the other, depending not on the various sizes and shapes it comes in but on something that nobody has ever been able to figure out. Pity. (This is fun. Let's try another one.)

All paragraphs are blocks of writing (words) printed (with ink) on pages (made of paper). Written words are symbols for units of speech. They are not the smallest units. There are smaller ones called syllables and sounds. In the other direction, words are organized into phrases, clauses, and sentences. Sentences are distinguished by the fact that they have capitals at the beginning and periods at the end. Several of these make up a paragraph, except in newspapers, where it usually takes only one.

Now in the paragraph above there is one word that destroys us. Except for that word, we could have neatly succeeded in writing utterly gratuitous nonsense. The word is "organized." There is no need to explain in full what the impact of organization is on paragraphing. But some few things have to be said beginning with the observation that organization begins in the womb. We organize ourselves biologically for the actualization of language, for the decipherment of the code of our language, for cognition, for observation, for speech, for listening, and finally for reading and writing. Lo, we are back to this moment and the paragraph, which is an organized assemblage of letters, words, phrases, clauses, sentences, and *meanings*. All paragraphs have these things. And here the similarity ends, almost. Not quite.

Let's say that there is one paragraph in the world that is a good one. If we took all the adjectives out of it, it would no longer be a good paragraph. If we changed all the nouns into different ones, or if we changed the order of the sentences, or, in fact, if we tampered with it in any way, it would no longer be a good one. What would we have done? We would have destroyed the multilayered organizational scheme of the paragraph. The adjectives belong where they were: a *childish man* is not a *man*; he is a *childish man*. The author of the phrase has organized the sound-sense signals to say *childish man* not something else. The sentences belong in the order of the original, not in some other order. A miniplay with just two characters and two sentences, one each, would be ruined if the wrong character spoke his sentence first.

FIRST CHARACTER: Yes, I have to use my teeth
                         to tie my shoelaces.
SECOND CHARACTER: I see you have only one arm.

But we have delayed long enough. What are the constants among paragraphs? What are the parameters? One is that paragraphs are sequences of structurally related sentences. This means that there are formal, linguistic elements of linkage. A paragraph with ten sentences does not have ten unrelated sentences. It has ten related sentences. One of these will have a sharply or widely focused semantic content. The others will deliberate on this idea by adding to it, subtracting from it, or moving on to some related semantic notion. The semantic core of a paragraph serves as a locus for the coordination of the details of the idea. Here is a simple paragraph that will hopefully shed a little light on these weighty propositions:

I saw a dog. It was big. It was black. It was mean.

Quite apart from whether this is a good paragraph or a bad one, it is a paragraph that has a semantic mass and a coordinated substance. All paragraphs have these two things. The word *it*, of course, is a dead give-away of coordination. The author coordinated *dog* with *big* and then with *black* and finally with *mean*. From another point of view, the author has placed the notions of bigness, blackness, and meanness in a secondary relation to the primary one of *dog*. First comes *dog*. Next comes *big* and *black* and *mean*. To use standard terminology, *big, black,* and *mean,* have been *subordinated* to *dog*.

Paragraphs exhibit both coordinating and subordinating techniques of composition. Coordinated paragraphs like the little one above are rare. They begin with a mass and then move on to a sequence of like structures, each one coordinated in the same way. Such a paragraph as the following is a coordinated paragraph:

This is my thing. I believe that an insult is an insult before the insult. I believe that love is only possible. I believe that the moment my son told his first joke was the best moment in my life. I believe that I have purposes sometimes, although I can't for the life of me figure out what the purpose of life is. I'll bet tomorrow will be just like today, only different.

The paragraph has a core (*credo*) and a yield. The yield is linear but symmetrical. That's coordination.

All paragraphs have a mass. Some have critical masses, others have not. Here is a pictorial mass with a high critical tension:

If we build in our minds a set of coordinate developments—a beggar's hand? the left-hand of somebody's god? a dead gesture of friendship? "This way to the balcony?" a hand reaching to scratch? —then we have mixed on an equal footing parallel potentialities.

On the other hand, if we move out from the mass in different directions, developing this and that as we go, which is what we usually do, then the "paragraphs" that we construct are described as having subordination. Here's one:

The first writing assignment that they passed in emphasized what many of those children were thinking and feeling. The assignment was to describe the way they felt about their school. As an alternative, I said that, if they wanted, they could write about the street they lived on or about the whole neighborhood or about any other part of town. Because of the miserable state their writing was in, and out of fear that they might not write anything at all if they felt

they were going to be lambasted, I said that I
wouldn't be looking at grammar or spelling or
syntax in the beginning but that I would be
looking for two things: (1) the richness and
specificity of details and (2) the openness and
courage with which they put their own most
private feelings down. Although I have taught
all kinds of writing classes since then, I don't
think that I ever again will receive such a trust-
ing and wide-open response.
                    JONATHAN KOZOL,Death at an Early Age.

The first sentence has as its mass *thought, children's thought, what
children were thinking*, and so on up to the first sentence itself,
which is the coordination and subordination of the elements of the
mass. The second sentence picks up *assignment*, develops it, and
subordinates it to the first sentence. The third sentence is coordinated with the second. The fourth sentence pursues *assignment*
logically by subordinating what the author's attitude toward the
assignment is. The last sentence backs up to a point somewhere
between *assignment* and *attitude* and logically explains the quality
of the *result of the assignment*.

One of the papers that was handed in, incidentally, was a won-
drously "coordinated" paragraph that began like this:

In my school, I see dirty boards and I see
papers on the floor. I see an old browken
window with a sign on it saying, Do not unlock
this window are browken. And I see cracks in
the walls and I see . . .

and kept going right like this up to the last of eight "I see"
sentences. The paragraph has no mass confined to any single sentence. Its mass is the sum of its parts, which is the way a lot of
paragraphs work.

We can generalize about paragraphs, then, and head back into the
matter of what to teach about writing. Paragraphs have semantic
masses that are usually expressed in a coordinated or subordinated
way in a single sentence, often the first. Paragraphs have development of this mass. The development is accomplished by way of
either the coordination or the subordination of the related and
deeper elements of the mass.

This is the easiest thing in the world to teach. A child can generate his own paragraphs in approximately the same way he generates his discussion. Of course, he doesn't have somebody interrupting him all the time, so he can go in a straight, unbroken line to the end. He can start with his mass *I came to school late yesterday*, and then he can quite formally, almost mechancially, latch onto the elements of this mass, the *I*, the *coming*, the *school*, the *lateness*, and the *yesterday*—and *tell* us what it was all about. He can come to understand that this is what everybody does when he writes (or speaks). It's merely a matter of hammering away at the words, the phrases, the clauses, and the sentences until they are all just right. With experience and practice, he'll learn that you can't leave out material that belongs, that you can't stick in things that don't, and that, in general, the success of his paragraph is directly related to his powers of observation and feeling. If he sees only half of what he is writing about, then his reader will get only half of it and will be left to wonder what the other half was like. If he doesn't feel strongly one way or the other about David Copperfield, then the passion in his character sketch of David is going to be nil.

Which brings us to an extremely important point in the teaching of writing, one with which there is not universal agreement. No child should ever be asked to write anything. The weekly or monthly composition is a menace of the highest order. It should be abolished from the face of the earth. Children should write only when they want to. Preposterous, you say? Not in the least. There is only one reason extant in the world why children should write regularly or from assignment. The reason is that that is what has been done. And there is no justification whatever for it. It has not worked.

It is enough to suggest, cajole, hoodwink, and otherwise bamboozle kids into writing. They can be sent to their desks or home often enough with burning desires to *write it down* without pretending, for some utterly inexplicable reason, that it is virtuous to write compositions on Fridays. There has never been a child who didn't begin his school days with an unbridled enthusiasm for paper and pencil. But there have been few indeed who made it all the way through school with that same enthusiasm. Somewhere along the way it gets killed. Usually on Fridays.

A New English classroom with teacher and students in it having a grand time exploring the worlds of language and literature and life is a place where writing lies cheek by jowl with talk and reading. The students write more often for themselves or for their classmates than for the teacher. (What kind of audience is that?) They write when they have something to write about, not when it is time.

In all events, if writing is to be taught at all, we can begin by noting seriously that it is directly related to language, although it is not itself language. We can let writing go where students let it take them. We can say frankly that one really good sentence a year is an occasion for great rejoicing. (Look at Frank's sentence! That is one great sentence! Let's have a party!) We can say that a dozen styles are better than one. In particular, we can say that a student's *own* style, the one he worked for ten years on, is infinitely better than all the accumulated monolithic styles of all the handbooks in all the worlds of men. We can examine existing writing fairly for its workings, and maybe even learn from the examination. And finally, we can suppose, until we are proved wrong, that the hard work of asking questions about how language and writing work and the harder work of finding meaningful answers to the questions will have some bearing on students' use of language whether in speaking, listening, reading, or *writing*.

Reading

Reading is in good shape. It has come from the Dark Ages faster than other things. And it's strange, really, that this is so, since it had to come much farther than grammar did. Whereas school grammar was mostly a harmless waste of time, "school reading" was downright harmful. It spent as much time on training the eyes to twitch right as on anything else: It supposed that the way to learn how to read was to start with letters, move on to simple words, then short funny phrases, and finally sentences. This was *before* Dick and Jane. But we have even managed to get those two behind us. And things are in pretty good shape now.

We can be very quick about it. Reading is *not* verbalizing what appears on a printed page. Many children can do that without having the slightest clue as to what they are saying. It is one thing to look at a sentence on a printed page, for instance, "Farmer Brown placed much importance on his crops," and then say it out loud. It is another thing to know what the sentence says.

Reading is *not* phonics and vocabulary study, although an intelligent phonics and an intelligent vocabulary study have their uses. In Chapter Four, the correspondences between the sound and the writing systems of English were discussed briefly. Here it is sufficient to say that there is a sound base upon which these matters may be taught, and that base does not include drivel like "When two vowels go a'walking, the first one does the talking." Pooh! As to vocabulary study, the old bugaboo of looking up the ten words listed neatly at the end of the study is safely behind us. Not that they aren't still there in many textbooks. It's just that New English teachers don't use them because they are wrong-headed. The idea was, I guess, that isolated words had meanings, which they don't.

The reader of this book should be able at this point to write his own paragraph on what reading is like in The New English. As a coherent part of the whole program, it adopts or adapts the principles of instruction for the teaching and learning about language, grammar, speech, literature, and composition. An analysis of what reading *is* is made by teachers and students. Its bearing on language, grammar, and literature is clarified. The complex but discernible characteristics of reading are investigated. And the result is an understanding of what reading is. Is it surprising, for example, that reading should be achieved by learning how squiggles represent certain events in speech? By discovering what the correspondence is between intonational features and punctuation practices? By learning to read by reacting to syntactic structures, the *same* ones that we use when we speak? By recognizing that meaning is the same deal in reading that it is in language? I hope not.

Literature, Composition, and Reading

The title for this last little section should really have been "Novels, Plays, Short Stories, Essays, Menus, Telegrams, Letters, Editorials, Advertisements, TV Programs, Radio Programs, Dreams, Themes, Notes, Sketches, Outlines, Précis, Biographies, Language, Grammar, Speech, Usage, Argot, Slang, Phonology, Morphology, Syntax, and the Kitchen Sink." For it is time for a big finish. Less frivolously, it is time to show by example how the many concerns of The New English are coordinated. Having done that, we will have come to the end of this introduction to The New English.

Elwood Prestwood reports in his "Using the New Linguistics," which appeared in the National Education Association booklet *Improving English Composition*, that recognition of the primacy of speech and language over writing has suggested a series of exercises that focus students' attention on what kinds of sentences they use when they talk. Students are brought to realize that the sentence patterns they use when they speak can be carried over into the writing situation. They learn by observation of their own verbal behavior that very many patterns of structure are used in speech. A joint effort by teacher and students is made to discover the value of using the patterns in composition, and to recognizing them while reading.

The whole effort has much to recommend it. The first advantage is that students come face to face with their own verbal language. But this is not all. Since language is not writing, the study of the linguistic structures in language behavior not only provides important insights into this behavior but serves as the logical base from which thoughtful, meaningful investigations of writing and reading can be conducted. Language is not writing. But writing is representative of language, or at least of speech. If the students can dissect their writing practices, a comparison to verbal activity suggests itself immediately. That they should use certain structures with good effect in speech but not in writing (with whatever modifications are indicated by the rules of the game of writing) would be shortsighted, to say the least. All together, the plan seems a sensible one. As Mr. Prestwood says, considering this approach to writing, "The instructor can use the principle of going from what is known to what is unknown, thereby improving the effectiveness of the learning to be achieved."

Coordination of the concerns of any English program as we have just seen in the case of language, writing, and reading, is a desideratum. You really have to try very hard to succeed in *not* coordinating things. A last shot for us brings together language and grammar, literature, reading, composition, and speaking and listening.

Here's a familiar passage from *Through The Looking Glass* that has delighted many a child for a hundred years!

There was a book lying near Alice on the table, and while she sat watching the White King (for she was still a little anxious about him, and had the ink all ready to throw over him, in case he fainted again), she turned over the leaves, to find some part that she could read, "—for it's all in some language I don't know," she said to herself.

It was like this.

Jabberwocky

'Twas brillig, and the slithy toves
Did gyre and gimble in the wabe:
All mimsy were the borogoves,
And the mome raths outgrabe.

She puzzled over this for some time, but at last a bright thought struck her. "Why, it's a Looking-Glass book, of course! And, if I hold it up to the glass, the words will all go the right way again."

This was the poem that Alice read.

Jabberwocky

'Twas brillig, and the slithy toves
Did gyre and gimble in the wabe:
All mimsy were the borogoves,
And the mome raths outgrabe.

"Beware the Jabberwock, my son!
The jaws that bite, the claws that catch!
Beware the Jubjub bird, and shun
The frumious Bandersnatch!"

He took his vorpal sword in hand:
Long time the manxome foe he sought—
So rested he by the Tumtum tree,
And stood awhile in thought.

And, as in uffish thought he stood,
The Jabberwock, with eyes of flame,
Came whiffling through the tulgey wood,
And burbled as it came.

One, two! One, two! And through and through
The vorpal blade went snicker-snack!
He left it dead, and with its head
He went galumphing back.

"And hast thou slain the Jabberwock?
Come to my arms, my beamish boy!
O frabjous day! Callooh! Callay!
He chortled in his joy.

'Twas brillig, and the slithy toves
Did gyre and gimble in the wabe:
All mimsy were the borogoves,
And the mome raths outgrabe.

"It seems very pretty," she said when she
had finished it, "but it's *rather* hard to understand! (You see she didn't like to con-
fess, even to herself, that she couldn't make
it out at all.) "Somehow it seems to fill my
head with ideas — only I don't exactly know
what they are! However, *somebody* killed
something: that's clear, at any rate —

If a class of six-year-olds or eight-year-olds or ten-year-olds exists
anywhere under the sun that would clam up or fall into a blue funk
given a dramatic recitation of this passage, bring the bulldozer and
cover them over. They're dead. There would be no point in a teacher
laboring satire and sadism in Lewis Carroll's *Through The Looking
Glass*. But a lively reading of the book, of this passage, cannot do
other than ignite linguistic and literary flames. Discussion will be
bright and animated. Some kids will demand equal time to give their
own readings. Little ones will wield their vorpal swords and go
whiffling all over the classroom strewing mortally wounded Jabber-
wocks in their wake. Older ones will write mock serious essays
entitled "The Killing of the Jabberwock," or "The Decapitation of
the Infamous Jabberwock; Being an Essay Upon Bestiality and Gore,
Wherein It Is Argued That The Slaying of a Jabberwock Is a No-No,"
or even "The Grammar of 'Jabberwocky'."

Some children will want to take out all the stupid words that
don't make sense and put in good English words. One will draw a
picture of the Jabberwock, and that will be his *composition*. A
group will put the whole thing on dramatically. They will write the
script, design the costumes, set the action, perform. The audience
will cheer the "beamish boy" and jeer the "Jabberwock," except for
one smart aleck who will do just the opposite.

One girl will go to the library to find out who this Lewis Carroll is, and she'll "report." Then somebody else will remember an Aesop fable or one of Walter de la Mare's verses. Comparisons will be made to "Jabberwocky" and then back again in the other direction, maybe this time to the nonsense verse of Edward Lear with its owls and pussycats in pea-green boats.

Somebody might pose a problem like this: Suppose you're a friend of the Jabberwock, but you can't get in touch with him except by telegraph. You want to warn him that the "beamish boy" is on the way to kill him. You send him a telegram, but you've only got enough money to pay for four words. What do you say? Everybody tackles the problem, and the best solution is chosen. Then, somebody picks up the phone, calls Western Union, and tries to send the telegram to The Jabberwock, c/o Jubjub Bird, Tulgey Wood, U.S.A. He reports on what the operator said, cleaning it up a little for classroom delivery.

Then . . . But the possibilities are endless.

Some will say that this is all silliness. I say that it is not. It is very very serious. But the seriousness doesn't necessarily show. In a New English classroom, language is the name of the game. "Language" is everything that was listed at the beginning of this last short section, and more. In an orderly fashion, from kindergarten (kiddie-garden) through the twelfth grade, language is studied fiercely. The English language is all that we have to talk with, think with, listen to, and read. If we do not know how it works, we will be its victims. If we do know how it works, we will be its masters.

POSTSCRIPT

For Teachers: There is little that I can say further to you, dear colleagues. It is you who have achieved this little book. Without you, there hardly would have been a New English. It is you who have done all the work. You have gone to the workshops and institutes. You have studied linguistics and the history of the language and the new rhetoric and all the rest and have made them work in the classrooms. You have thrown out all the materials and techniques that didn't work; you have created new material, new techniques, new curricula, new practices of all kinds that are fair to our profession and useful to students.

We know that The New English is better than the old. It is not musty. It is not simplistic. It is not remote and foreboding. It is the best that you have been able to devise. And as the work on it continues, it will get better. We are learning more and more about how people learn natural languages and how they use them. What is even more to the point, we know that there are some dandy ways to teach English in school.

None of it is easy. It is all very very hard. Our work is harder every day: we must know more, read longer, study harder than ever before. Our students, too, are not sliding through their classes. No

more frittering for them. The demands are so great that we sometimes shrink before them. So many journals to keep track of. So
many reports. To say nothing of all the jazz that we have to put up
with—the committees, the hall monitoring, the paperwork, the PTA,
the Union, administrators, school boards. But still, after a martini
and a good night's rest, we come back to go at it again. Why?
Because the kids are there ready to break their pencils over our
heads. They didn't get to talk about Paul Simon's poetry yesterday
because they had to tape that demonstration lesson on transformational grammar. But today, they're going to talk about it or know
the reason why. (But I jest. Or *do I?*)

For Parents: Contrary to the opinion of some people, The New
English is not part of the International Communist Conspiracy. The
most insecure among us react the most violently to change, any
change. It wouldn't matter if the whole world thought it was a good
idea to change something; they would adamantly resist. And that's
all right, as long as they don't go around shooting people they don't
agree with. Anybody would rather have a name hurled at him than a
stick or a stone.

The New English has won the enthusiastic support of the students
and teachers who have brought it into being. They have found it
intelligent and challenging. As a program, it offers a sequence of
planned lessons that are designed to light up our linguistic world.
With the lights on, our children can *see* language in its myriad shapes
and uses. Just as a person walks around and around a free-standing
sculpture, peering, crouching, studying, to *see* it all, to understand it,
students "walk around" language *for twelve years* studying it. The
"grammar" that they study makes sense. The "writing" makes sense.
The "literature" makes sense. It all makes sense because "making
sense" is the only thing that The New English cares about. Whatever
doesn't make sense is rejected by teachers and students alike.

The new English *is* political. If it is not a part of the International
Communist Conspiracy, which it definitely is not, it *is* a part of the
National Democratic Conspiracy. The rock of our national being—
freedom, individual rights, tolerance, equal opportunity, social responsibility, diversity—is the soul of public education. The endur-
ance of our form of government and our way of public life depends

in large measure on what is happening in our schools. As a creation of government, the public schools are *for* the people. They are just as much for the parents, for us, as they are for the students. Our active interest and concern in what our children are learning in school is absolutely necessary to the preservation of our way of life. If *your* school district is using The New English and you are opposed to it, then you must get over to the school and state your case. If the district is not using the program and you support it, then get over there and ask why they are not using it. If you don't care one way or the other, that's your problem. Your kids are either bored to tears in English or they are all charged up. We'll get to the bored ones sooner or later. We'd just rather have your help.

INDEX

CHECKLIST OF
RELATED READINGS

BOLINGER, DWIGHT, *Aspects of Language*. New York: Harcourt, Brace & World, 1968.

DIXON, JOHN, *Growth Through English*. Reading, England: National Association for the Teaching of English, 1967.

HOGAN, ROBERT E., (ed.). *The English Language in the School Program*. Champaign, Illinois: The National Council of Teachers of English, 1966.

MULLER, HERBERT J., *The Uses of English*. New York, Holt, Rinehart & Winston, 1967.

ROBERTS, PAUL, *The Roberts English Series*. (6 vols. Grades 3-8.) New York: Harcourt, Brace & World, 1966–1967.

SHUGRUE, MICHAEL F. *How the "New English" Will help Your Child*. New York: Association Press, 1966.

SQUIRE, JAMES R., *A Common Purpose*. Champaign, Illinois: The National Council of Teachers of English, 1966.